James Bridgwater has gone out of way to get a black cat Kiki to replace Alice this year as they are discriminated against. He will be working with Project X at Plymouth Theatre Royal Creative Learning Department and Symbiotic Theatre. Having self-published the novel *Masterstroke*, he is working on *Blind Justice*, a novel about a transvestite vigilante with mental issues.

Dedication

To individuals who are unorthodox

James Bridgwater

CONFESSIONS OF AN EMOTIONAL SHIPWRECK

Copyright © James Bridgwater (2016)

The right of James Bridgwater to be identified as author of this work has been asserted by him in accordance with section 77 and 78 of the Copyright, Designs and Patents Act 1988.

All rights reserved. No part of this publication may be reproduced, stored in a retrieval system, or transmitted in any form or by any means, electronic, mechanical, photocopying, recording, or otherwise, without the prior permission of the publishers.

Any person who commits any unauthorized act in relation to this publication may be liable to criminal prosecution and civil claims for damages.

A CIP catalogue record for this title is available from the British Library.

ISBN 9781786123251 (Paperback)
ISBN 9781786123268 (Hardback)
ISBN 9781786123275 (E-Book)

www.austinmacauley.com

First Published (2016)
Austin Macauley Publishers Ltd.
25 Canada Square
Canary Wharf
London
E14 5LQ

Chapter 1

My first confession is with regard to why this book lacks an introduction, preface or foreword. I confess that previously whenever a book had a prologue I always skipped it automatically without giving it a second thought. However, once I was a short way into my degree in Literary Studies with Theology and Philosophy I soon discovered that these preliminary pages often contained very useful information with quite detailed synopses and, as often as not, a good bit of character analysis of the principal individuals in the story. This became more and more helpful the further into the course I got.

While at university most people I discussed it with said their biggest problem with essay writing was keeping them down to the maximum word limit. It was usually 3000-3500 words, and points would be deducted if the piece was seriously lacking or excessive in wordage. I didn't want to seem lacking in intellectual ability so I always used to agree, saying "Yes, it's like pushing sardines into a tin." I would have loved to know just how many of them were telling the truth and how many were just playing an academic game of Keeping up with the Joneses. I had to do all I could to scrape together enough information and knowledge to get within a couple of hundred words of the lower end of the demand. I doubted that the tutors ever actually counted anyone's piece to see if it was accurate, but they gave the impression that they could get a fairly precise idea by counting the number of lines written on. They seemed to have an equation similar to x words per line multiplied by y lines per piece of writing. So if a piece had, on average, sixteen words per line and forty eight lines per page it was roughly four and a half pages for a three thousand five hundred word essay. I developed a very long winded way of expressing myself in writing which I'm sure my lecturers had noticed yet nobody mentioned it specifically. For example what could be put as, "Hamlet was dead." became "At this point in Shakespeare's dramatic text the character of Hamlet is no more amongst the living, but has passed on to join his father (and previous King of Denmark) where hopefully they are both now resting in peace rather than rising from their graves as troubled spirits." We had to put our word count on the cover sheet with various other data required by the markers in a very specific format and all work had to be word processed which had various pros and cons in my opinion.

I had been given a word processor by a friend of mine who had upgraded their system in what was the technological tsunami of the time, although that was a considerable number of years ago now so at the time nobody knew what a tsunami was unless they were familiar with Japanese art from a few centuries ago. However the machine I was given was not a PC and so it used a different system which could not be integrated with the college computers, so at the start of each essay I had to commit myself to working at home with all the distractions that entailed such as my friends, who were very keen on binge drinking - as I was - but had no education to attend to. Alternatively working in college offered different diversions such as going to the Counselling Centre, where they had drop-in times scheduled and it was the only place I knew on campus that supplied free coffee and played Classic FM. On good days they also had distinctly pleasant oils and incense to give my nostrils an experience equivalent to that which I had in my ears, listening to a mellow piece of baroque chamber music. There was of course the chapel right in the heart of the whole site where there was a fair chance of free coffee, and if there had been an ethnic evening the night before I could frequently find a cold, damp bhaji or a slice of pizza wrapped in Fairtrade, Eco-friendly, Save the Dolphins kitchen paper. Whichever refuge from scholarly action I took they both often had people who were keen to discover the problems in my life and help me overcome them, either by prayer or very dilute psychotherapy. This was a conclusion I reached having had numerous encounters with religion and psychiatry in my past, but I'll tell you about some of that later in this document. Before I go any further I think I need to present chapter two of this book, as the confession it contains will be relevant and significant to the entire volume. Also, I think it is the kind of information many writers would have put in their preface, but as I admitted at the start of this section I haven't given an introduction as I never used to read them, so why should I expect you to do so?

Chapter 2

If I had not decided to write this book as I have, with no preface or introduction, this would have been chapter one and the last chapter would have been the prologue but I can too easily imagine people reading books as I used to and as I can't count on them having had a time of literary study to correct this bad habit I have to slide everything along by one chapter.

My confession in this chapter is with regard to the truth, contents and nature of this entire work. I am not stating that this is an autobiography, but also it is not a work of fiction completely composed in my imagination. What I am proposing is to write a story in which all individuals, events and activities are not necessarily recorded and reported exactly as they occurred, but everything and everyone is rooted in reality. People's names will be changed as I am ignorant on the subjects of libel and slander and I do not wish to upset or anger anyone, but place names will probably be maintained. I remember when I did a year at Manchester Metropolitan University studying psychology we had a particularly interesting lecture on "Truth and its Perception". Clearly everyone sees things slightly differently for numerous reasons. Fundamentally there are points such as when people are standing in various spots so they physically view things at a different angle and I remember my best school friend was colour blind which I was perpetually fascinated by. What was emphasised in the lecture was more to do with the recording of data, for example if I see a car crash and in my statement to the police put "the car banged into the van" it is assumed to be travelling slower than if I write "the car smashed into the van." Letters and words have always seemed far more intriguing to me than numbers and figures and this is an example of why. It also explains why I like good poetry so much as each word has to be selected, analysed and confirmed to be the correct piece of vocabulary for that line.

Thus this book is not attempting to be a gospel, but nor is it a completely fantastic world with as much reality as "Lord of the Rings". What I admit to doing is in general I will record things as I recall them but a few points may be exaggerated and emphasised while one or two will be toned down and less stressed. Also the aspect which I am going to say I think is most likely to be faulty is the time line so I will say now that basically there will be progress in a chronological manner, but if things are not quite in the correct order I apologise for that now. This however leads me to wonder just who I am apologising to and to whom I am confessing. I suppose the apology is to anyone that recognises themselves in this, despite being shielded by my use of a different name, and the confessions are to anyone who wants to take them on board. I'm curious regarding the idea of "going to confession" which the Roman Catholics do but as will be made clear later I have always had more connections to the Church of England from quite a young age. Most of my life my dad has been my confessor while I was the confessant, but from about the age of eighteen I took a very cynical view of the truism "honesty is the best policy." This is because I believe being truthful got me a three year prison sentence and a millstone round my neck for the rest of my life which has been one of, if not the most frustrating, aggravating things I've ever known. However the confession linked to that is deeper in the volume so if that has stimulated your curiosity you had better read on.

Chapter 3

If I could recall anything of the first five years of my life I expect there would be events and actions which took place then that were worth confessing to, but unfortunately my memory is like a *tabula rasa* up to the time of just after my fifth birthday. However *tabula rasa* is probably not quite the right term as that means a blank slate which has never had any information upon it and is waiting to be used for the first time whereas I think the memories of my first five years are simply locked away and at present are out of my reach. It is the event of shortly after my fifth birthday which has gone a long way to leaving me an emotional shipwreck, which I believe is a fairly accurate way to describe my emotional condition. This is despite numerous psychiatrists and other similar people who have tried to help me overcome the problems induced by this major trauma.

One beautiful summer day in 1977 my mum had picked me up from nursery school and was driving me home to our little cottage in the village of Holt near Bradford-on -Avon. We came round a sharp hairpin bend coming down a hill on a road my mum was quite familiar with, yet for a reason which I have never discovered the car went out of control. Being so far in the past the idea of it being compulsory to wear seatbelts was not even floating in people's imaginations at the time, so my mum went flying through the windscreen and I went forward from the back seat and hit the seat in front of me which only resulted in me getting about five stitches in my chin. However my mum was not so fortunate.

The only mental picture I have of my mum in my memory that does not come from photos I have seen since is seeing her lying face down on the tarmac about five metres in front of the car. The car had rolled over and if I recall correctly it did in fact end up back on its wheels. I can see the image in my mind as clearly as if it is a picture right in front of my eyes. It is as clear as if it had been burnt into my memory using a high power laser beam. She had thick, wavy brown hair which I inherited as I can see when I look at photos of her, and I have her eyes too. She was wearing a brown skirt with a white blouse. The whole scene with its backdrop of thick green vegetation beyond the roadside crash barrier is framed by the rim which held the windscreen in its place. What happened after that is a bit of a mystery as I think I must have passed out then and I presume a car came along shortly, found the scene and so drove to the nearest point of communication and called for an ambulance. Yes, this was in the dark ages of communication when the phrase "mobile phones" would probably have made people imagine a number of phones hanging on bits of coloured thread, as likely as not over a baby's cot. My next memory is from a short time after that when my dad, who was working for the Royal Navy at the time, was sitting in our home's main bedroom with me on the side of the bed. How much time had elapsed between the two scenes I really have no idea but it was probably the next day or so as my mum died shortly after being taken to hospital.

This memory of Dad and I sitting on the side of the bed upon a candlewick bedspread is a very strange one, as I can see it in a way similar to how people describe near death experiences. People say they are looking down and they can see themselves on the bed with the medical staff frantically doing all they can to bring them back from the point of no return. I can see myself and Dad sitting on the side of the bed as though I am looking down from the top corner of the room. At the time and for years afterwards I never gave a thought to how it was for him, as telling me my mum was dead must have been one of the worst things he ever had to do. The idea was emphasised to me much later when I made friends with somebody who was married for over twenty years, till his wife died of cancer and he had to tell their two children their mum was dead. In some ways I think he had it better as they saw it coming as she faded away over six months rather than going from 100% to nothing in less than six hours. However what made their situation so bad was that his children were older and so they still remember their mum, whereas is it happens early enough you just can't remember anything of the person in question.

Obviously if you can't remember someone you can't feel the same degree of loss at their not being present any more. I believe this is my case - the memories are there but an emotional firewall has come down blocking all access, though I do occasionally wonder if hypnosis would get me anywhere. Yet I remember being angry for years after, because he told me that everyone else in the family knew and I was the last to be told. I felt that as she was my mum I had a right to know first. Looking back now I'm sure everyone did all they could for me, but I couldn't see it at the time. Having been a naval officer family for generations, stiff upper lips and keeping such weak things as emotions to oneself was inbreed by now so once my mum had passed away it was almost as if she had never existed. She was never mentioned and I don't recall any pictures or photos of her anywhere in the house though I think Dad had a little bedside photo.

However the aspect of it all which as likely as not caused me the most emotional damage at the time was that, as the car had crashed on a dry road, in perfect light conditions, with no other vehicles involved I needed a cause of the accident and only one made sense to me. I must have distracted my mum or at least done something to cause her to stop giving the road all her attention and give some to me. Thus there were years when confessing to feeling responsible for my mum's death was not beyond me. I think if such a thing happened these days a person with any connections would be overwhelmed with e-mail addresses and mobile phone numbers from bereavement counsellors.

Then, once I was old enough, I went to boarding school and for the first time in my life I now feel self-confident enough to confess to some of the things that went on there. I know that a lot of people have ideas about the homosexual goings on which are supposed to occur in English public schools and I can't deny that they do to some extent but I would think that the principal difference between the truth and the perceptions of outsiders is the extent of it. However if one went to a school which had a homosexual/paedophilic master I imagine things would be on a different level. I get the impression from Roman Catholic priests in the news recently that schools run by them with names such as St Patrick's are rife with such actions but again it is probably due to media magnification and is nowhere near as prevalent as it appears. There seem to be various dark corners to the picture of what happens to children who spend any length of time in an environment separated from their parents. In a wide range of situations I have been told various tales by individuals that have grown up either in care, in boarding schools or even in establishments run by monks or others where one would think that their claimed religion would keep their morals in order. We were in school for terms of about twelve weeks or so with no contact with the opposite sex except via Matron, a couple of the teachers and the dinner ladies. The ages of seven to eleven are definitely a time of discovery and exploration in all fields of life, so looking back now I think we might have been abnormal if we hadn't done the limited sexual exploration we did.

It was also very much a time of discovering limits and boundaries with regards to friendships and other types of behaviour. The first thing I really remember with regard to time at boarding school was the way I used to get frustrated with all the "cry-babies". We would arrive at school over the weekend before the first Monday to have time to acclimatise to being back at school and being away from Mummy and Daddy back home. I used to enjoy my time at school as I had few friends back at my home village so I had a much better time with my mates at The Old Ride Preparatory School for boys. However, even the senior boys walked down the long wooden corridors with a tear in their eye on the first night back. I had seen the ashes of my mum buried in the ground and my father was to become somebody who seemed to only cry once a decade, so emotion became to me a contamination of my thought processes. Back then I would probably have made a quality Vulcan if I had been dyed in indigo and had points added to my ears by cosmetic surgery. I was so unimpressed by these weaklings who used to cry about being separated from their parents, that if they were in my year or below I used to pick on them. I must confess one of my favourite games was to pick a victim for an hour or so and chase them round the empty classrooms, along the lengthy corridors and into the dormitories as they filled up, and creep up on them by using the back staircase. One boy who was particularly unfortunate was Colin. I don't know why I picked on him so much but something made me decide he would make a fine pin cushion and I used to harass him with the pair of compasses from my geometry kit. They had nice short points so I could push them in his chest, arm or back without having to worry they would go in too far and cause serious damage.

However that resulted in a quite surreal experience about twenty years later that certainly taught me a good lesson in fate and coincidence. Back in Plymouth where I have spent most of my life as we moved there when I was about ten (which is why I was boarding at the school in Wiltshire). One day I needed to go to the doctor, I can't remember what it was for but nothing too serious. After sitting in the waiting room getting more and more bored and fed up with the way patients who arrived after me went in to see the doctor before I did, when the receptionist called me over and asked if I would mind a medical student sitting in with the doctor during my consultation. Being keen to get it over and done with I probably would have agreed to sit in front of a whole lecture room of trainee doctors so I said it was just fine. Following that I was directed to Consultation Room 3 and with a sigh of relief I went up to the door. It was always possible the student was a nice looking girl and she might wanted to feel various parts of my body so it might work out to be to my advantage as at that time I was very jealous of my friends who had girlfriends and especially the ones who had got beyond holding hands.

I walked in the door and took a seat as expected, seeing the back of my usual doctor leaning towards the screen behind which I could the silhouette of someone arranging things on a wheeled table. Then the doctor turned, smiled and said, "Afternoon James! Sorry to have kept you waiting but Colin is doing a placement with us here for a week or two." So out came Colin, the poor sod that I had used as a victim on whom I released my post maternal death frustrations, mixed with my pubescent angst.

I froze in my seat. He was there with access to syringes, scalpels, and a wide range of other instruments which had not been designed for torture, but improvisation was a definite possibility. Never mind what he could inject me with. It was probably one of the most distressing moments I've ever had in a doctor's surgery but it was clear he had become a doctor because he wanted to help people and he was above holding grudges against petty fools such as me. Fortunately I was unaware of the activities of Dr Benway back in those days, as some of his remarks and comments in

Naked Lunch would have been very distressing passing through my mind at that time.

"While in general I avoid the use of torture- torture locates the opponent and mobilizes resistance-the threat of torture is useful to induce in the subject the appropriate feeling of helplessness and gratitude to the interrogator for withholding it. And torture can be employed to advantage as a penalty when the subject is far enough along with the treatment to accept punishment as deserved."

Chapter 4

It would have been around my time at Prep school that I learned how things which at first appeared to be an affliction could be used to my advantage. Obviously once it had soaked in to me that my mum was dead and that was the end of that matter - as I could do nothing about it and it was a fact as unchangeable as the form of atoms - I realised it did however provide me with a very playable sympathy card. Also the car accident brought on epilepsy which may have been on its way anyway or may have been induced by the crash. So my confession for this chapter about life in boarding school is that this allowed me to pretend to have fits. Most of the teachers at boarding school were quite acceptable and easy to get on with, especially Mr Hamilton-Legget who became head of the science department after I had been a pupil for a couple of years. Hammy-Legs as he was known is probably one of the individuals that most aroused my interest in science, particularly with the project I volunteered to do at weekends to combat boredom. This was to go through the school's entire microscope slide collection and put them in order as then they were completely chaotic. So I spent many pleasurable hours looking at everything from sheep's testicles to dogfish brains and in the plant section all from cactus water storage cells to seaweed floatation sacs.

The one teacher I hated in the whole school was Mr Birch who taught music (the recorder) and looked like Robinson Crusoe would have if after many years on a desert island he had his hair washed, conditioned and dyed black but not cut. He had a black beard halfway down his torso and waves of jet black locks that used to hide his face when he conducted with too much gusto. He scared me witless and so almost without failure I would exercise the same ploy before each weekly music lesson. The class took place in the gym which was an annex attached to the main school building round the back.

The attractive country manor house at the heart of the school concealed a mess of annexes, parked vehicles and the corridor connecting to the gym. Getting to the gym involved numerous little sets of a couple of steps and multiple corners which made it easy to find myself separated from all the others on their way to be educated by the Mad Musician of Borneo. It gave me the chance to lie on the floor and tell the next passer-by I had just had an epileptic fit and so needed to be taken to Matron. Thus I would be laid in the sick bay and told to rest for a period and see how I felt then. This was certainly very convenient. I'm amazed nobody noticed the regularity of it, but maybe they let me get away with it as I was top of the class in just about every other subject.

Another thing about faking fits and still having a few real ones was that about once a month Matron took me to see the local paediatrician which was boring in itself, though it may have been on a day I had a test or something which would be advantageous. The really good thing was that Matron drove a yellow MG Spitfire and was very familiar with the local country roads. These made lovely day trips, and Matron and I got on well. I think she felt sorry for me being 'Mumless' and if I recall correctly she had no kids of her own and so that was one reason she was so happy to work in a boys' school. Just enjoy the company of a crowd of seven to eleven year olds, then she could get them off her hands as they turn into teenagers; a very good scheme.

I don't seem to have got on well with any music teachers. At my secondary school we had to line up in a corridor before music lessons waiting for Mr Hutch to come along and unlock the music room allowing us to enter. He was a man who would have benefited from anger management, not that I had heard of it back then. His nickname was 'Epi' as when he was upset he used to erupt like a volcano and become the centre of a danger area. 'Epi' was short for epileptic as he was considered to have a sort of fit when agitated. I certainly had evidence of that due to a foolish move I made once while in the music room corridor. Mr Hutch walked passed me and then suddenly focused his attention on a pupil just down the line from me. Being a bit of a class clown and enjoying nothing more than making my classmates laugh I decided to put my hand up behind his head with two fingers raised in a 'V'. Obviously I wasn't as behind him as I thought as he saw me do it and so exploded. He spun round and grabbed me by the neck and pushed me against the wall. I was glad he was just a small, weak man as otherwise he'd have lifted me off the ground as Darth Vader does when an officer of the Empire fails to catch Princess Leah.

The principal building of the Prep school was a converted country house and had a very appealing, impressive appearance from the drive and the Front Lawn which pupils were not allowed to walk on. I imagine The House of Usher which Edgar Allen Poe narrated the fall of looked pretty similar except that property overlooked a small ill-fated body of water.

We students had to get up every morning but Sunday for a pre-breakfast run round the Front Lawn and then turn back at the Grounds man's cottage to come down the avenue of lime trees and then breathlessly make our way to the dining hall which had walls covered in school badges. There was a shield for each establishment with their motto and emblem on, similar to the ship badges my dad lined our hall with. There was one each for each school a pupil had progressed to. I remember Plymouth College for boys was already on the wall and the one with the most appealing name was Giggleswick High School.

Going out on a frost coated morning could give some memorable images to a young boy exploring much for the first time in the world of experiences and emotions. I recall one morning particularly clearly. I heard the Headmaster's shoes crunching the grit behind me as my house mates and I got in position to start the daily run. I surveyed the scene ahead, half admiring the poetic beauty, half questioning its reality. Surely only the Master painters could create such mesmerising sights. A backdrop composed of staggered layers of heights plummeting to valleys, gorges and foothills. All cloaked in mist, uniting with the subdued clouds to shroud the cobweb embraced flora. Thus peregrination could not be expected without bequeathing paths as obvious as comet tails on the Front Lawn of diadem dressed grass blades. The drops of dew hung frozen on the tip of each blade like a collection of diamond chandeliers for the ants and aphids waltzing to the Butterfly Ball.

Over to the far left beyond the lime tree avenue was the pavilion which sheltered the arcane grass cutting and rolling equipment. Even older than Mr Wilkes who had the biggest swelling on his head I could imagine - not a hair on his scalp but a permanent lump at the back, above his ear which was almost a pink golf ball. Back then I was unfamiliar with words like tumour, cyst and carcinoma so I thought it was a bruise which had refused to leave after being caught off guard by a cricket ball. It was when that happened to someone else I saw the worst accidentally inflicted bruise I can think of, which still sends a shiver up my spine when I think of it. Gavin Douglas enjoyed a sunny summer afternoon as the shadows began reaching out and the temperature became comfortable rather than too hot. The red leather sphere of pain dropped out of nowhere as he came round the pavilion corner. An Olympic gold medallist marksman with a cricket ball gun couldn't have got a more perfect shot in his eye. He had to go to hospital as rapidly as possible to try and save his eye and I expect the pain needed serious relieving too. Days later he returned to school with a white eye patch over a truly black eye.

I passed the 11+ and Plymouth College entrance exam with what felt like flying colours. Taking the exams had been a peculiar experience as being the only pupil trying to get into Plymouth College I sat the exam by myself. For some reason I did it while sat at an enormous dining table in the Headmasters part of the house.

Chapter 5

When I was in the boarding school dormitory I think I developed some routines which have become so ingrained in my lifestyle they are practically addictions about thirty years later. The first one which comes to mind and which I have almost become obsessive about is not going to sleep in a silent room. Back in those days I shared a bunk bed with my friend Lance Jenkins; myself on the lower level and him on top. There were about twelve bunks in the room so there was always someone having a chat to one of their neighbours, or if not that, numerous people talked in their sleep so there was always a background murmur of sound. One event relating to that which also stuck in my memory and was brought to my attention a number of years later was when we listened to a tape of *The War of the Worlds*. This was the musical version by Jeff Wayne based on the novel by H.G. Wells and narrated by Richard Burton. I had already read the book as I greatly enjoyed science fiction and fantasy in those days, and that would have been when I read *Lord of the Rings*. Our dorm was never a silent room, therefore I got used to falling asleep with a blanket of sound as well as a duvet. When I went home to compensate for the absence of twenty young boys in the room with me I listened to Radio 4 and after the shipping broadcast and the national anthem I became aware of the World Service. Since then I've used this information source to keep myself up to date with international activities and events. I have often found being unable to sleep a tiresome dilemma but at least at boarding school I found a productive way to pass the time. I used to take a piece of foolscap to bed with me and rip it up into pieces the size of two postage stamps. Then I'd chew them up individually getting each one in to mulch which I rolled into a ball. These balls I left on my locker to dry and so in the morning they were rock hard pellets. These were terrific peashooter bullets, as all the other boys just fired a blob of mush which would splat on an archaic desk or blackboard. If it hit someone it just made a damp mess with no real effect. If I hit someone with one of my shots they reacted as if they had been stung. If I hit bare flesh the victim would give an aggravated "Ahh," and spin round looking for an assailant. If timed properly and with the correct victim I could get some very memorable results. The best ever was when at close range I hit Paul Caswell just after the whole of 5B had been told to shut up and get on with the maths exercise.

"Oww! Shit." Then he gave a burst of coughing and spluttering trying to conceal his accidental interjection. Within seconds the rest of the classroom were making a range of curious noises as they tried to subdue their laughter. Mr Lewis spun round and glared at Paul with such intensity his neck vein must have been very close to bursting and I'm sure his eyeballs expanded their diameter.

Back in those days family genealogy was not what it is today and I've always found mine somewhat confusing. I certainly can't tell you for sure how most of my relatives got to meet each other and where they were living or what their occupation was at the time. I think a little look at my mum's side of the family tree will be beneficial now. My mum's parents were ex-pats who lived in Africa and I know her dad Andrew was an airline pilot who had to stop being one due to an alcohol issue. His first wife, my grandmother, was an enthusiastic smoker who died due to pleurisy and was keen on a drink or two as well I believe. I've never been sure but

I feel that the condition of an addictive personality exists and that they had it and genetically passed it on to me. They divorced and both remarried so at that time they were all still alive I had three sets of grandparents. When my mum died we pretty much lost contact with my blood grandfather and his son, my uncle Sean. We used to exchange Christmas cards with the latest family news and that was about all. However these days we do seem to be back in touch with Sean at least, but it's not easy as he is now a sheep farmer on the edge of Perth, Western Australia.

Somehow, somewhere, my blood grandmother was lucky enough to meet a very successful Birmingham chemist who made his fortune out in Africa. Back in the days when apartheid was in full swing and Rhodesia was the name of what is now Zimbabwe he made a lot of money from skin whitener and a mouse to straighten curly black hair. He made enough money from selling his company to a large pharmaceutical chain that over the years he has held the following properties, not quite all at the same time but always a good few at a time. He had a flat in Pimlico with a Rolls Royce to cruise round in, a Mombasa beachside mansion, his own hotel in the Seychelles, a Geneva penthouse, a lodge in a Kenyan game reserve, a villa in Bermuda and an estate by the Thames where he keeps his Bentley. For years he has spent his time enjoying these and travelling from one to another on the top of the range cruise ships.

He, Harold is a very generous individual and has always been incredibly kind to me and my dad even though we are only connected to him by marriage. In the days I was at Prep school he used to invite us up to spend a week or two with him in London in which we always visited Hamlyn toy store and I used to feel so important as he always called me Mister James.

One year when I was about ten he invited Dad and I to come and join him in Kenya for a holiday. We were both very eager to go out and explore the Dark Continent and pick up some unforgettable memories. We flew into Mombasa airport early in the morning just as the sun was coming up over the horizon. First we saw the clouds take on a gilt look and then, as we came over the city there was an intricate patchwork of quickly shrinking shadows surrounded by a shockingly strong light. It would have been about six thirty when we got off the aeroplane and it was already so hot that I remember asking my dad if it felt as it did because the jet engines were still giving off heat as we walked behind them into the arrivals lounge.

We were met by Grandpops as he was known and driven through the city on an exceptional journey. I remember now as clear as crystal a couple of things I encountered then. Firstly we drove past some local stores which had lepers lying, begging outside. This was a blatant exhibition of suffering unlike anything I had ever seen before. Young black men with limbs missing and faces worse than anything I'd seen in any horror films but loathsomely real. It was back then I still wanted to present the equivalent series to 'Life on Earth' when I was old enough. That TV series showed incredible images of worldwide wildlife and now I was going to see some of it with my own eyes. After we drove along the main road and under an archway of fake elephant tusks over a dual carriageway we entered the more suburban streets and approached the high class residential area. Here most houses had swimming pools, even if they had direct beach access as well. The sides of the streets were lined with serious security walls occasionally interrupted by automated gates and the grass verges were populated with giant land snails and land crabs. Like most things in Africa these creatures are on a rather different scale to that which we Europeans are familiar with.

We ended up at a villa on the top stretch of beach which I've since learnt is near the area where the men from the Armed Forces used to come when on leave from anywhere in the surrounding region including places as far away as Aden. The house had a number of servants which was something I felt very uncomfortable with as I wasn't used to telling people what to do. The gardeners, cooks and housemaids were alright as they kept out of the way and didn't need to take instructions from me. What I felt awkward with was having an African equivalent to Mr Hudson from *Upstairs, Downstairs* lurking in the corner of the room waiting to fetch a chilled Coca-Cola at my discretion. I thought it would be easy telling someone else what to do but I never got used to it. The house had its own swimming pool but the sun was so burning hot that we just couldn't go out in it for a good few hours in the middle of the day. Also if we used the pool just before or after the middle of the day we needed to use flip-flops as the paving slaps got so heated that walking on them was quite sufficient to burn your feet. The owners had a collection of pets which thrived in the tropical climate. There was a big brown male Burmese cat called Rangoon after the capital of Burma. My dad's Burmese cat at the moment is a female ball of energy that loves to chase and catch mice and birds whereas out there it was a diet of curious insects and small lizards.

The house was so near the beach that it just took five minutes' walk over dazzlingly bright white sands, through a labyrinth of prickly pears to come out to a private bit of seashore. Then from there you could proceed into the sea and explore a reef with all the shimmering fluorescent colours I had seen in films about the Great Barrier Reef. Fortunately there was a bit separated from the Indian Ocean by the reef coming up and reaching the water surface, which made a sizable lagoon type area which the sharks couldn't get into. Despite it being a neighbourhood which many people said resembled at least one idea of paradise, we did have one unpleasant experience there. My dad and I were having a swim having come down in just our trunks and loose cotton short-sleeved shirts, coloured almost as brightly as the coral and sea life with African patterns and designs. We left them on a rock when we went in the water and Dad left his sunglasses and watch there too. When we came back after our visit to the kaleidoscopic aquatic flora and fauna we found that all we had left waiting had been stolen to be sold to make a poor Mombasa resident a few more shillings. It was certainly a place where people would do anything and everything to get money. In the part of the city which equated to an open air version of Plymouth Pannier market there were countless stalls selling soap stone sculptures. There were greatly stylised figures of Maasai warriors, and all the native animals, jewellery, chess sets and basically anything the locals thought the tourists might like to buy to take home and show off at the next cocktail party.

I've always appreciated good food and I was quite surprised by some of the things we had to consume while in Africa. The first thing which caught my attention was breakfast, which was fresh pawpaw followed by bacon and eggs. Harold had a few English habits and traditions which he was planning to stick to, regardless of what the Dark Continent could throw at him. While out there we regularly had seafood and a large quantity of steak, as cows are the prime animal farmed out there. Maintaining Englishness is such a thing for him that he will import a turkey, sprouts and Christmas pudding with brandy butter and has them on 25th December even if it is in a remote lodge in a Kenyan game reserve. He has also gone to the trouble of having a snooker table shipped out and reconstructed in the lodge. It was the only place I've ever been where I could see a herd of elephants pass in the morning of Christmas Day and then have a traditional seasonal meal for lunch. This could then be followed with a frame or two of snooker once someone had ensured we didn't have a Green Mamba under the table.

It would have been while I was at Prep school that I first developed my interest in literature and so acquired a taste for poetry. A principal factor in this would have been my English teacher, Mr B. (This isn't just what I'm calling him for the book but that is what we called him at school as he had a long, hard to spell name so he was Mr B. to all his pupils.) He was the teacher who introduced me to John Masefield's "Sea-Fever". As I've been living next to the sea since my dad moved from the village outside Bath to Plymouth when I was about seven, its start has become one of my most quoted lines; "I must go down to the seas again, to the lonely sea and the sky, and all I ask is a tall ship and a star to steer her by." Another thing which boosted my poetry fascination was that the school had an annual speech day service where top pupils got up on the stage in front of parents and the whole school to read out pieces of work and once I read a poem I had written about a hedgehog. My confession for this chapter is that I am so proud of my knowledge of literature that I get very shirty with people who quote verses but quote them wrongly or misinform their audience with regard to the author. Two occasions in which this has happened stick in my mind predominantly.

The first occurred at the boarding school and so helps with my attempt to maintain at least a hint of chronological order. One evening my friends and I were lolling around in our pyjamas on our dormitory beds. We were discussing the good and bad points of our new headmaster. He had only been with us a few weeks yet already had been labelled with the nickname Naff - I'm not sure but I think that was because N, A and F were his initials but it may have been just to describe his character and personality. Looking in a dictionary now I see the word's definition includes: inferior, worthless, an incompetent. This certainly was the way we saw him, particularly after the following event. He came in to turn off the dorm lights and tell us we would be in trouble if we had any pillow fights or midnight feasts as it was still near the start of term so we were still charged up with energy and our tuck boxes still contained numerous sherbet lemons, home-made cakes and other goodies.

How we got talking about it is a mystery but the subject of the problems caused by money was raised, with regard to pocket money as likely as not. Naff got us all into bed and walked towards the light switch saying, "You know what the Bible says don't you boys? 'Money is the root of all evil.' That's something for you to think about." I have always been impressed by people who quote the Bible using exact chapter and verse references to back up their statements but as I said if people misquote things I'm happier if they shut up and say nothing. This happened to be the only line in the Bible I knew with pinpoint accuracy and so just as he reached for the light I called out, "That's not what it says, Sir. It's the 'Love of money which is the root of all evil.' Have a look in the first letter of Timothy, Chapter 6, and Verse 10." I knew I was right and particularly satisfying was that I knew he had no escape as I was sure there was a Bible in the room as at the end of the list sent out to tell each school boy what was requisite for each term was always listed a copy of the Revised Standard Version of the Bible for R.E. lessons.

One of my roommates jumped off his top bunk and had a copy of the indisputable text in his hands before Naff could think of an excuse for misquoting the famous epistle. He leafed through the tissue thin pages at hell for leather speed and almost instantly had the incriminating line under Naff's nose, which was at it happened his predominant facial feature. He then proceeded to look down his prominent snout at me, my roommate and the text with disdain and walked out saying we would be in serious trouble if we didn't go straight to sleep.

The other memorable quotation correction I have is nothing like as satisfying, as it wasn't correcting somebody who ought to know better. It was with a long term friend and drinking associate of mine and unlike the previous event it took years to prove who was right and who was wrong. The piece of literature in question was 'The Tyger'. I could have forgiven someone if they thought it was 'The Tiger' as that was an understandable error but saying it was written by Rudyard Kipling was disgraceful and infuriating. Especially as this was a lady who had been educated at Oxford Girls School according to what I had been told. We regularly drank together in each other's homes or in local parks in more favourable weather; before binge drinking and ASBOs were even conceived. We usually started off in favourable frames of mind, but frequently parted company with a poor relationship, having had a heated debate on the authorship of the poem and our social skills and memories having been corrupted by cans of Super Strong lager. One day however, knowing I would be seeing my argumentative opposite Tina later in that day whereas usually we just bumped into each other I took a copy of 'A Choice of Blake's Verse' with me to resolve the matter once and for all. Once we had met up at her house and were settling down to a relaxed smoke and drink in the midst of her multiple cats I waited for the entrance of the cat Tiger Lily and then raised the issue by asking if the name was spelt with an 'i' or a 'y'. She said it was an 'i' of course, why should it be a 'y?' Then I extracted the volume from my pocket and showed her the page with the poem starting, 'Tyger! Tyger! Burning bright in the forests of the night...' Being the lady of good character that she was she admitted defeat and some years later I took care of some of Tiger Lily's offspring (Alice and Shekinah) when Tina had to move into a flat which didn't allow pets.

Chapter 6

The infuriating thing about starting school in Plymouth was that all the students there seemed to have been generously supplied with intelligence by a postcode lottery. I had expected to be at the top of the class as I had been before but I found I was middle to bottom and yet I was still trying just as hard. There were more subjects to manage as science had now been divided down to biology, chemistry and physics. In the language of first year students this was life, elements and the difficult one. I remember talking to my dad about the hard one which had been Natural Philosophy in the age he had done it both at schools Stubbington and Berkhamsted and also as part of his engineering degree in Glasgow University, very closely linked in with John Brown shipbuilding yard where his placement was done.

The trouble with postcode lotteries is that it's not optional to join in, it's compulsory so I can't choose not to take part. Also around this time of my life I discovered that most decisions for a teenage school boy with one parent are made for him. However I found out that I could choose to express my feelings by writing them myself. The difficult bit was deciding who to show my sentimental scribbling to as I was at a boys school and I felt the other boys were on a different emotional level to me. This meant that I am now confessing to having a piece of poetry hidden away for years before it was revealed to anyone and then it slipped out by accident. This was written because for a long time at my new school in Plymouth I spent a considerable time reflecting on my previous educational experiences, including the vague, faint memories I had of St John's Primary school, which was a nun run establishment. Events there had prompted me to write my first significant piece of poetry:

Mothering Sunday

Sitting at our desks at St. John's Infant School,

It's that time of year again when everyone makes cards.

Hearts or flowers or cuddly bunnies to take home to their mums,

Like a cloud on the horizon I've seen it drawing near.

Teacher brings in sheets of card and glitter, pots of glue.

They all know what they want to do; they're stuck in straight away,

But then I catch the teacher's eye and think I see her flinch.

My eyes go down; I watch the floor and scuff my shoes again.

She comes and puts her arm round me, it feels a little strange,

"Why not make your dad a card? I'm sure he'd like that James."

I feel more than uncomfortable and I make a poor attempt.

Jealousy, resentment, anger, grief and pain, triggered by a mum's day card.

Generally I do like cards, I'll send or I'll receive.

But ever since a barrage of "Deepest Sympathy,"

And other sent condolences, dad's dictionary helped there.

Now hating mum's day cards, I'd burn them. Cremation once again.

  One reason I was reluctant to display my poetry in those days was that everything was handwritten back then and unless I gave the task my sole undivided attention I had handwriting which left a scrawl on a piece of paper which looked like the trail of a paraplegic spider under the influence of alcohol. One thing which gives me relief when I'm feeling guilty for having such bad handwriting is that I know one member of the clergy who has got himself a doctorate yet writes in such a fluid style that words link up across the page. He is someone I admire despite giving me advice which needs explaining, such as when I asked for a tip on giving up smoking he said, "Don't give up!" This meant don't give up trying to give up.

Chapter 7

I expect most people like myself have some things they did at school which might well be eligible for a confession but I did things which got me caned on a number of occasions, plimsolled, rulered and planked too. I'll go into the details of some of those in a while, but first tell you about my great success regarding corporal punishment. I escaped ever being caned by Judge Jefferies. He was the terrifying deputy headmaster who stalked round the corridors of the over a hundred year old boy's educational establishment. He used to wear his big black gown with his cane down his sleeve and a mortar board covered in chalk dust concealing his receding hairline. It was a school of tradition and some of the names etched into the desks probably belonged to men who had gone on to be commanding officers in both world wars. They would principally have been naval as back then you could be a naval midshipman at 14 with a trip to Dartmouth's pride and joy, Britannia the Royal Naval College. My family has a very strong naval history, with at least the last three generations all having been naval officers and I get the feeling one of my distant relatives was at least at Trafalgar if not on HMS Victory. I have a little piece of memorabilia which I'd like to take to the Antiques Roadshow which is a little barrel bearing a plaque carrying this statement, "From the teak of HMS Iron Duke. Admiral Jellicoe's flagship. Jutland 1916."

Back to my assorted antics which got me hit by various tools by a number of masters. I'll confess the most memorable and significant was in one of my years boarding in Colson House. I was in a dormitory with three other boys who were just as mischievous as I was if I remember right but also with three mice we had bought at the local pet shop. We were in a dorm which, unlike most had a sink in so we could give our mice drinks and they were happy to share our tuck box contents for their fodder. As it happens this was also a dorm where we could climb out of the window and manoeuvre on to the roof for a secret cigarette but the mice were what we got caught for. One day we came back to the boarding house after classes and found the boxes they had been in were vacant yet there was no sign they had escaped.

It was revealed to us once we were all back in the room that a cleaning lady had been doing her job when she was distressed to hear something rustling under one of the beds. We had been sensible until then and remembered to put the box holding the mice into the wardrobe so they weren't found. We felt we looked after our mice very well and we used to exercise them on the portable record player which was used as their treadmill when not using it to play albums such as Iron Maiden's Powerslave. Back then we still believed stories about the drum kit being smashed up at the end of a concert and cymbals being thrown like Frisbees from the stage and decapitating members of the audience. It was about the same time Judas Priest was taken to court in the States for concealing satanic verses in their lyrics.

Other things which got me corporal punishment were far more basic, fundamental things such as talking in class or failing to do homework and so are not as interesting. One thing which I must confess I did get away with was a real achievement. It was the French lesson we managed to break down to complete disruption. What happened was we bought some proper glass stink bombs which I don't know if you can still get now. We took one and placed it under the foot of the teacher's table on the platform at the front of the classroom. Then when she came in and put her books down on the table the glass cracked and the highly odorous sulphur dioxide began evaporating into the atmosphere so that, despite opening the windows and trying as hard as possible to ignore it we had to be evacuated from the classroom after about five minutes.

One thing which I would gain from greatly later in my life was the fact that over these years I became very familiar with passing time in an English public school as later on I would find out how correct Evelyn Waugh was with what he said in *Decline and Fall.* "Anyone who has been in an English public school will always feel comparatively at home in prison. It is the people brought up in the gay intimacy of the slums, Paul learned, who find prison so soul-destroying." That relates to a later incident though, so you must continue reading to find out about what I did to get a life long criminal record which is an intangible millstone round my neck in the ocean of the job market.

Chapter 8

I can't blame my dad for not being the answer to all my parental issues as he hadn't had an easy time as a child with a father in the navy, back in an even less emotional era. He was however fortunate enough to have a sister. The closest I had to a sister would have been Alice of Looking-Glass and Wonderland fame. In the early years there just were no girls around. I'm thinking of the time I was boarding at The Old Ride Prep school which was an all boy's school in the middle of the countryside so we never got to see anyone. It really was 'Never-never-land' as far as contact with the opposite sex was. Then after that to Plymouth College which did have girls in the sixth form back then but has since had a dawn of reasoning and the girls have infiltrated the entire system from top to bottom. Boarding for two years there obviously didn't help my 'interpersonal boy to girl skills' and by the time that was over I was seventeen in the lower sixth form. This contained attractive and unattractive girls, boys who had been getting familiar with girls for the last decade, boys who had at least communicated with girls of their age who weren't family members, the boys who were painfully shy round girls but knew what they were trying to do. Then there was also me.

I had always been painfully shy, even round people who I knew and who knew me. For example I've two cousins I'd meet about once or twice a year. He was a couple of years older than me and she was one or two years older than him. They both had the single sex school education as far as I know and did grow up in a remote village in deep, dark Hampshire. However, knowing each other and their sibling's friends they seemed to know how to handle members of the opposite sex.

Back then I would have grasped any straws if I thought they would help me on that front. This was probably an influential reason for my initial going to church. Not the only reason by any means, but a significant factor. If I could meet a girl or two who were at least close to my age bracket I might be able to get myself together enough to ask them if they wanted a cup of tea and biscuits or a glass of squash. The church used to thrive on social events over the proverbial sandwiches, mini sausage rolls, flans, crisps, vol-au-vent and cheese and pineapple cubes on cocktail sticks. However due to bad luck, a curse, or God moving in mysterious ways, I had numerous free lunches with little progress on the relationship front.

Back then the St. Paul's church, or at least its vicar, was involved in the majority of my social activities. At Christmas the more adventurous of us and some work friends would always go out and do something a bit foolish and memorable. It was common to do whatever it was each year on Christmas Day morning which seemed to habitually be a time of dazzling sunshine yet biting cold wind straight from Siberia. I remember one time we went to the local tourist site where people go to watch the coming and going navy vessels and so wave them off. It's a spot called Devil's Point and in the bleak mid-winter it can be hellish, even if with extreme cold rather than fire and brimstone. I wouldn't be surprised if one of my local heroes of the past used to go there in preparation for his mission. I'm talking about Captain Robert Falcon Scott who was born just up the road from where I am in Keyham at this moment. A place called Outland House which is an appropriate name for such an explorer. Another famous explorer from Plymouth was Fernaux who was the first recorded Englishman to do a circumnavigation of the world both ways. He lived in a place called Swilly Manor and is buried in the graveyard of the church I attend nowadays. The name Swilly, which means 'farmland', has had a much greater influence on the area than the name Fernaux. Swilly is a colloquial term for a particular area of Plymouth which had about the worst reputation of any part of the city. The title for those who are born and bred Plymouthians is 'Janners'. Despite having lived in Plymouth most of my life, I spent long enough growing up and being educated in public schools that I don't sound at all like a Janner.

Back on a Christmas Day in the blowing gale, we came out to have a barbeque and 'the bravest of the brave' went for a dip in the Hamoaze (a stretch of water where the River Tamar and Plymouth Sound unite and which separates Devon from Cornwall). What social workers, members of the clergy and devoted members of the community will do especially if it's to raise money or awareness was quite shocking sometimes. This had been just 'for the hell of it' and what happened later in the year was particularly impressive. It was a noticeably chilling winter and for some reason the homeless had particularly made the local news. I think The Big Issue had opened up their local office or something had happened to bring the unfortunate in to focus for more than just the Salvation Army. What Rev. John, my dad Mike, and social worker Bob did was take on the role of being homeless vagabonds on the streets round where they lived, including in front of the church. As the vicar was taking part, the Church wardens couldn't throw the little group off the church grounds. Thus the little group had a place to build themselves a shack and so went to the local shops and asked for cardboard boxes, pallets and basically anything which could be helpful. They received enough material for a two man shelters, so two could take cover while one stood outside. That was very trying till they were given an oil drum to set up a fire in. Thus whoever was outside could at least keep warm and try and dry off. Next came a saucepan from 'God knows where' and they received bones from the local butcher so as to make up some broth. The greengrocer donated his scraps and shreds to give it a bit of body and so they had 'something to eat'. Being an area with a good community spirit they had company most of the time and particularly around midnight. This was because the church they were in front of was just a car park away from the local pub 'The Royal Marine' which had a reputation across the area if not the whole of Plymouth. It was run by a man called 'Rocky' who had certainly been a boxer in the past and used to set up a ring in the pub garden for the locals to have competitions in. If possible I'm sure he would have had it with bare knuckles. The garden of my house was separated from the pub grounds by a wall of laurel trees so we didn't see anything but heard it all.

The church and the pub were fine as neighbours most of the year but at Christmas it did become a bit trying sometimes. This was because the regulars would go in to the bar as early as possible on Christmas Eve and start lubricating their vocal chords with alcohol. Then at about quarter to twelve they would stagger across the parking space and fall in the back door of the church to attend Midnight Mass. Treating them as we would want to be treated being part of the basic Christian dogma they didn't get thrown out but were sat down at the back to slur their way through all the Christmas carols they recognised. Depending on the vicar's sermon quality and length they may or may not fall asleep in the back pews by the end of the service.

I must confess that it was around this time I enjoying being 'a star in the intellectual firmament.' This was how our teacher of RE would address us at the start of every lesson. I didn't know any other school which had its own chapel and chaplain. For the first few years Religious Education was a compulsory subject which we had to do once a week. It was done in Room 1 which basically was the Reverend's room. Not that I ever studied it but it was the room where one did Spanish too as that was also taught by Father Andrew. I have distinct memories of things which happened in there during our RE lessons. Not that I really noticed it back then but I think it wouldn't have been far off to call the subject CE (Christian Education) as I don't remember touching on Buddhism, Judaism, Hinduism or any other belief system.

One memory which has stuck in my head is that we had to learn the first 13 verses of John's gospel by rote. At the time I had no idea I would go on to do my degree at the age of twenty-eight rather than just tow the development line as I planned and expected at the time, i.e. Birth, nursery, primary school, prep school, secondary school, university for 1st degree. Then the path splits and the academic faction go on to do a masters, doctorate and finish off with a professorship writing books on their favourite texts, taking a lecturing tour of the States once they have their children on the pedagogical pathway. Meanwhile the more physical faction, those who played for the school teams in their spare time, are out sailing their own boat or walking round playing golf. Personally in the days of my RE I would rather help the Head of the English department put on a review show at the end of Christmas term, then a more contemporary piece such as *The Long, The Short and The Tall* or a revised classic in the spring and the obligatory Shakespeare in the summer. What I mean by a revised classic is taking a story or tale known to all and then rewriting and updating the script. The archetypal example of such was when we took the tale of *Pilgrim's Progress* and put it into modern language and gave our devils and demons sharp suits, dark sunglasses and pencil line moustaches which were added to the older looking ones in the makeup department. However I didn't feel comfortable in the makeup room as people kept asking me if I was wearing mascara and some people said I looked like a girl with my flowing dark hair down to my shoulders. This feeling of discomfort deterred me from going back to the makeup department when I changed my costume and became an angel rather a demon. Thanks to not having any facial decoration removed, unlike everyone else I was the only angel with a pencil line moustache that night, and of course it was the night my great aunt and my dad were in the audience.

Clearly my flowing hair had been passed on from my mum as I could clearly see from photos I had inherited her eyes and hair. Being a fashion victim some of the time in the 70's, she's seen in numerous pictures wearing a beehive. I get the impression hairstyles and appearances meant a lot to her as my dad had to remove his beard for the wedding in full Naval uniform, leaving the church under an archway of officer's swords. I have no memory of what my dad looks like without a beard as after getting married he talked to his commanding officer at the first opportunity and so got permission to stop shaving, rather than to start growing facial hair which is the way the Royal Navy goes about things.

When I was growing up, I passed through the trials and tribulations of adolescence in a family of one child and one parent with two cats. I think I would have grown accustomed to shaving early every morning if I had an example to follow. However I spent a few crucial years as a weekly boarder during that period and even when I was at home on Sunday mornings Dad was probably up and out to the church just round the corner before I was out of bed; I went to the only school I've ever heard of that had Wednesday afternoon off and compensated for it with lessons on Saturday morning. To my knowledge even Mr Wackford Squeers's Academy; Dotheboys Hall didn't do academic work on Saturday mornings.

Some events which involved me crossing the chaplain's path were when I indirectly started on a very long and circuitous route to my confirmation. It all began when I got together with a couple of boys that shared a dormitory with me and we decided to study ghosts and the like. In itself that was OK, but it led us on to things such as Tarot cards and Ouija boards which was where the trouble started. Firstly a couple of us bought a pack of Tarot cards and a got a book with instructions on Teach You How to Read Tarot cards. There were basics such as ask a question, shuffle the cards and cut them. Then get the answer from whichever card comes up. Also we learnt how to spread out the cards in particular shapes to read peoples past, present and future. These things we would do during the day for members of the boarding house at a small charge such as two cigarettes, a good chocolate bar or a packet of biscuits. We only did our Ouija board readings in our dorm after lights out. Quite how it worked I don't know but I'll confess to being responsible for the movements some, but not all of the time. We had a board with letters of the alphabet around the edge and also two points marked 'Yes' and 'No'. I can't remember how we got caught but I think one guy was so scared by something that came up he had to talk to an adult about it. Whatever happened, the chaplain was informed and came down on us like the Massachusetts Puritans did on the Salem witches in *'The Crucible'*. It didn't mean anything then but did later as in my degree I studied *'Death of a Salesman'* having done the job myself for a while so I seemed to copy some of Miller's play subjects in my life.

Chapter 9

One of my "crimes" which makes me feel particularly pleased with myself as it required a degree of planning, organising and sticking to my schedule regards a very good friend of mine who for the sake of anonymity I shall call S.P. for the moment. Now I'm inclined to say friends come in a wide range of categories. To start with there is the principal division which separates 'true' friends from acquaintances. Proper friends are the ones who will buy you a beer despite having bought the previous one and being aware the chances are they're buying the next one too. However there's no denying pseudo-friends can and will do this on occasion, but the difference is that a real friend will not make some sarcastic comment or sneer at you over the rim of the pint glass they've just got.

I think my upbringing has had a major influence on this but I find that a considerable majority of my friends are significantly older than I am. I did have a very good friend, my best friend at the time who was in the same year as me at school; but beyond him nearly all good companions are older than me. My friend Spence first talked to me because our names put us next to each other when we sat in alphabetical order. I often wonder if we would have established such a strong affinity if we had sat on opposite sides of Mr Nelson's classroom. Certainly once we had demonstrated our regard and respect for each other and disregard for rules and regulations we were often told to sit on different sides of the room by various teachers as they thought we would be more manageable if separated.

Getting back to the next confession on the list; what did I do that involved S.P? She came into that significant range of individuals who I call family friends. I suppose that's just a way of saying that I liked them and my dad liked them too. S.P. and her husband had first got to know us as we lived at the end of a cul-de-sac, number 32, while they lived just along at 28 if I remember rightly. My dad was ex-navy as I've already mentioned while S.P.'s partner was a member of the Forces who was sent to patch up the wounded squaddies and matlows at the Falklands conflict. They had two children; Andy who was a year below me and at a different school, and Beth who was about three years below me and was quite happy being a tomboy with us rather than having to stay at home with her mum learning all the girly things of life. S.P. was given as much support as my dad could give her to help her through the period of time in which she didn't know what news the next phone call may bring. Would it be another idiot trying to sell double glazed windows or would it be the dreaded call from the Ministry of Defence by which 'the next of kin have been informed'. I don't remember much about what the adults did back then as I was busy being a teenager which was daunting enough at the time, but nothing compared to my perception of the angst of 21st century adolescence. As my dad had never really tried to form another partnership with anybody after my mum died, I guess in a way S.P. was a bit of an adopted mum to me as I regularly went and had meals with the family, and looking back now I can see she was everything I would have wanted my mum to have been. Unfortunately I can't compare her to my mum as I have no memories of the kind of person my mum was and she's not a hot conversation subject, except previously between me and my therapist/counsellor. When the Falklands was finished he came back home with no physical injuries but probably having seen some sights to make him ask himself some serious questions about mankind and humanity. The family decided to move to a small town in the country and he joined the G.P. practice there for an income. Despite the distance between us we kept up good contact with each other using the only services available then: real snail mail, postage stamps and visits when possible; even if just made when passing through.

This would have been around the mid 80's when Dr Who was only watched by children hiding behind the sofa unless they were feeling especially fearless, and it hadn't become a subject one could take a PhD in, as it is now. That was when Longleat had a Dr Who exhibition and we went to see that as much as the lions and we didn't expect to see Lord Bath being hassled by a TV crew from This Morning trying to persuade him the estate was due for an industrial size makeover. I'm drifting again; back to my well planned misdemeanour.

When I was at a Plymouth boy's school with quite a reputation in the area we had to choose how we wanted to occupy our Tuesday afternoons. We could join the cadets linked to any of the Armed Forces or take the Duke of Edinburgh Award scheme. For some people it was a very difficult decision but it all seemed pretty obvious to me what I should do. Not going to join the navy cadets as that would probably lead to getting cold and wet and I doubted the real navy would take on someone with epilepsy, so what was the point in training for something I could never achieve? No point joining the RAF cadets as from what I'd heard they spent nearly all the time in classrooms and then once a year got to go up in a glider which they would have control of for ten minutes if they were lucky. Now maths was never my strong point but I knew enough about equations to see that one didn't work out. The D of E awards were the option for all the wimps and the kids who didn't have any grandparents and so needed to find a way to get used to dealing with elderly people. One of my sets of grandparents had divorced and then both remarried so I had an extra set of grandparents, but as all the ones on that side of the family lived in Africa back then it didn't make much difference. Anyway I was lucky enough to have a terrific great aunt who I saw on a regular basis and back then I still had a great grandmother who lived to be ninety-two or so which meant I was quite familiar with the more mature members of society.

Thus I was driven to join the army cadets which meant I got to dress up in a very uncomfortable green shirt, wrap my ankles in puttees - a fashion accessory the Indians had sensibly given up on years ago - and try and polish the toecaps of my boots so I could see my reflection well enough to shave in it. On the good side I got to run about with a .303 Lee Enfield rifle and fire blanks while out on Dartmoor. Occasionally, about once a term, I went to Tregantle firing range and got to fire REAL BULLETS from an SLR and a Bren gun. Then once a year about thirty of us went to a real army camp for a week in which we stayed in the barracks six nights and had one night out under canvas waiting for the fire fight that would be lit by a parachute flare. For anyone reading this that has never had the pleasure of standing in a wooded area in the middle of the night with a few small camp fires nearby as a parachute flare falls to the ground, let me give you a few words. As the shadows of the trees are perpetually moving across the ground, and are being cast by an eerie white/blue light coming from an unusual angle it seems as though the whole floor is alive with snakes interlocking with each other as they do at the bottom of a pit Indiana Jones would cringe at. Just to add a bit to the description which will only help a few individuals I expect; it's similar to the way a carpet with a Paisley design on appears in flickering candlelight when one is being strongly influenced by LSD or psilocybin. Also on our 24 hour expedition we got to eat genuine army rations which I enjoyed, particularly the readymade porridge which already had milk powder and sugar in; it just needed water adding and bringing up to temperature to simmer for a couple of minutes.

These days in some circles my nickname is Rat or Ratty but considering how devious I was regarding my project to see my friend S.P. I deserved it then. Originally it started because I was born in the year of the rat according to the Chinese calendar, and one birthday I was given a fine bone china mug with all the details of a rat's personality and their characteristics. The first year I was in the cadets we went to an army camp in Hampshire in a warm, sunny summer. It was one of those summers in which my greatest enemy was the pollen in the air due to my hay fever. It doesn't matter how much time, effort and energy you have put into your camouflage if you sneeze just as the enemy are entering your vicinity. I'm not too sure about the order of the camps after that but I know I went to one at Oswestry, one in the dark depths of Cornwall and a second one in Hampshire. The one thing I really recall about my army camp in Cornwall is that I got up in the middle of the night from the Nissen hut in which I was barracked to go out for a piss and probably a cigarette too as likely as not. I crept over the floor and opened the door as quietly as possible and then stepped out in to what at first appeared an alien landscape. Fireflies! That was the only night of my life I've ever seen them and it became imprinted in my memory. I was reminded of the sight a few years later when standing at the top of a slope and looking out over Glastonbury festival campfires at about three in a morning.

There was another army camp set for the Brecon Beacons. It would be a lot of outdoor activities such as hiking, canoeing, abseiling and other pleasant, relaxing pastimes. Now I think it was after then that I canoed down the River Dart in early February with a retired Royal Marine and some other cadets at a time when there were icicles on the river banks. I had a wet suit for that escapade and still lost feeling in my limb tips. I read the other day it's an urban myth that Eskimos have 40 words for snow; maybe it's words for cold.

So returning to the devious Rat. I decided I had done enough army camps by then but it was a long time since I had had more than a short chat over a coffee with my friend S.P. and I wanted to rectify that. So I told dad I had signed up for the army camp and he would need to pay for the travel expenses and sign an insurance disclaimer which he did without a second thought. I got there on the coach with the other cadets, the NCO's and the officers to find it was even colder and wetter than I expected. However, to make my scheme convincing I needed to tolerate the conditions for about 24 hours which I did. I now confess that on the second morning I lied, saying I was too ill to get out of bed. I needed someone to look after me and I couldn't travel as I was. This looked to be a major problem for everyone involved. However I mentioned I did have a friend who lived just down the road and she could pick me up at her town's train station; all I needed my cadet friends to do was get me on to the train. Yes, as it happened I did have her phone number with me by chance so I could call her and, being the terrific person she was, I'd be ninety nine point nine percent sure she could put me up for the rest of the week.

I used to particularly enjoy staying with her family in the mornings as there was never any pressure about time to get up, and once I did I went downstairs to be greeted by what was a magnificent breakfast by my standards. At home I usually just had whatever cereal had been cheapest at the local supermarket and that was it. At this household there was a cornucopia of cereals including a selection of mueslis followed by an abundance of bread types to be adorned with a profusion of preserves. What always used to be the ultimate perfection to this ideal breakfast was that Radio Three was played in the background so Bach Cello Suites accompanied a fabulous start to the day.

Therefore when I stayed for a few nights without any warning I was coming I had a top start to the day, and even if due to premade plans I was left in the house by myself I was quite happy as there was a marvellous record collection to sift through and a library of top quality literature.

Ironically, while on another stay at this great home from home I also had one of my most unpleasant mornings. The night before I had a wonderful supper composed of quality beer beforehand and wine during the meal and in the cooking. Stuffed pheasant or something similar with a speciality of the house 'S.P's Red Cabbage'. I don't usually follow up recipes but this is one that I have, being the most splendid red cabbage I've ever known. However, I must admit what may be seen as gilding the lily is that I've added cashew nuts to the Bromley apple, mixed spices, orange peel, molasses brown sugar and TLC to personalise the dish.

I had got up during the night to relieve myself and had an epileptic fit in the bathroom, during which I hit against a porcelain toilet roll holder and cracked it. I then must have fallen against it as I gave my back a cruel gash without realising it and then I returned to bed. A few hours later I awoke in a damp, sticky bed thinking I must have wet myself or something. So I moved to get out of it and suddenly felt a stabbing pain in the vicinity of my left kidney. I then opened my eyes and, looking at the quality linen sheets, I found they had gone from sky blue to burgundy and I was reminded of the scene with the horse's head in 'The Godfather.' Once I confirmed I was alone in the bed, not accompanied by the head of the pet dog, I composed myself and went to see my 'adopted mum' in the neighbouring bedroom. Once she assessed the wound it was decided I needed suturing and so went to the local A and E where Dr Payne obliged.

Stays at that household always introduced to me cultural phenomenon I would not have discovered otherwise, such as a double album by the string quartet Kronos who played a fantastic version of Purple Haze by Jimi Hendrix, and Dinner Music for a Pack of Hungry Cannibals by Raymond Scott. It really was an artistic, educational centre and it is the only house I've ever been to which isn't owned by the National Trust yet has a harpsichord in one of its rooms. The bookcases were lined with an enlightening range of texts, from an anthology of graffiti to classics such as Kafka, Dickens and Durrell.

Chapter 10

It would have been around this time I first encountered what in chemistry lessons was C_2H_5OH, ethanol. I remember I had a low opinion of the simple poison after our paths had crossed just a few times. However back then I had no idea just what I was dealing with and these days I've since seen a number of lives completely corrupted by it and I've already been to at least one funeral which I believe it was one hundred percent responsible for. Also I know at least one person who is on the same road and it's looking like a one way street for the person I have in mind. The first drinks I got familiar with were Thunderbirds and Scotsmac. I used to meet up with two friends from the other boarding house and we managed to combine our money and so get a bottle from a dodgy little general store down on the Barbican. I reckon the law was the same back then about buying alcohol when one is underage or giving the money to a gullible stranger. This was always particularly practical when buying cigarettes as they could be given one in return for the favour. We would offer a swig of the bottle to anyone who obliged then but it was about the time of the big televised AIDS campaign and so there were a lot of rumours and sick jokes going about. Because of this people wouldn't share a bottle with anyone they didn't know and trust and some people wouldn't even go two's on a Marlboro or a spliff as they started appearing on our scene about that time. I must confess that as I got people to buy drinks and tobacco for me when I wasn't old enough, I occasionally do it for local teenagers these days.

One of my most memorable early encounters with alcohol took place out on Dartmoor with a friend of mine I knew particularly well from 'A' level biology class. We had to do some research for a practical piece of work and so a number of students and one or two teachers got access to a cottage just outside Princetown, home of the famous Dartmoor prison. My mate Justin and I managed to get to the shop in the town, persuade the shopkeeper we were over eighteen and so bought some cans of Strongbow cider. It maybe we didn't convince him, but he was glad of the extra business as it is not a commercial strong point being one of the most remote settlements in Devon and Cornwall. I don't know where its nearest police station is and in the 1980's teenage drinking was in a different league to what it is now. My friend and I took our cans and found a nice little 'Sleepy Hollow' in which to get inebriated. I remember two cans each was more than sufficient back then.

I wish I didn't have the tolerance I have now as the other weekend on Saturday I had three pints in a local pub then three cans in a friends flat just up the road from my place. To follow that we then shared a bottle of a wine and concluded by having about a bottles worth of wine from a box. All the time we were at the flat the whole lot was intermingled with a range of cannabis specimens and a selection of music from You Tube. My trouble with this friend of mine Paul is he is too generous for his own good and, unlike a number of proud people I know, I don't have a problem accepting charity. Also I feel sympathy for his situation, as to maintain an adequate income he does an unpleasant job at a most disagreeable hour. He works in a factory bending and moving sheets of metal from three in the afternoon to eleven at night and has done so for over ten years. This would be an unenjoyable way to work for anyone but I think he finds it especially nasty as for years he lived in Africa and so grew up in large, open spaces. I think he has a very restricted social life as he hasn't got a good friendship with any work mates. They usually keep each other company as a lot of them are Eastern European, as most local taxi drivers are these days. Certainly recently a number of shops have opened up in Studentville and Union Street which is world famous as the site sailors go for R and R which is adjacent to Millbay. That is the red light district which is plastered with used condoms, needles and empty white cider bottles.

Chapter 11

As I've mentioned I had a psychological breakdown in the middle of the period in which I was sitting my 'A' level exams. The only subject I had sat all the papers for was the general studies and one out of three papers for each of the sciences. What happened really was a very strange thing, pretty much out of the blue and I'm not aware of anybody else having had the same sort of thing occur to them. So here it is.

I went to bed one night in the season of taking the exams, but without having to get up and take one on the coming morning. I can't remember much about that evening but I expect Dad had done me a good meal for supper which we would have had around eight o'clock. We always ate round that time rather than having high tea at six-ish as to us tea was a light refreshment served at half four composed of china tea, homemade chocolate cake or toasted crumpets soaked in hot butter, and quite possibly some biscuits. After supper's main course and then either some cheese and biscuits or maybe yoghurt we would have sat and watched TV for a few hours depending on what was on. M.A.S.H and Hill Street Blues were both popular series in those days which we would each watch from our own positions. My dad would be sat on a white leather rotating chair, probably with the brown Burmese cat Brum on his lap and browsing through a book or a newspaper, giving it less attention as the evening went on. I would have been lying on the sofa which made up the large part of the three piece suite that was now off-white/cream and had, over the years, provided three cats with good claw exercise facilities. I can't remember it but I imagine it was a very impressive suite when first acquired yet by this time the leather was clearly much abused dead cow skin that had slipped through to a decade in which it was really quite out of place. I would be watching the Hill Street undercover members of the NYPD and always enjoying the sergeant finishing off his morning briefing with, "O.K.! Let's be careful out there!" I think I would have liked my dad to say that to me when I started walking to school every morning as I always did, never a lift or bus money. At the time I used to get quite annoyed about that, especially on Tuesdays when I had to take in my army cadet uniform as well as all my books. However now I'm very thankful I got used to walking everywhere.

That fateful night we both went up to bed in the same way as usual, without much conversation as I feel we were each waiting for the other to say something like, "I'd like to apologise for the other day. Don't you think we could sort things out if we took the time and trouble to talk about them?" However I wasn't going to break the ice by saying that very difficult five letter word, and it was round this time I started listening to the beautiful first album of Tracy Chapman. Lyrics such as; "Sorry, is all that you can't say, years gone by and still, words don't come easily, like sorry, like sorry." I can't be certain but it's something I did for years and years every night so I'm almost guaranteed that once in my bedroom and listening to Radio Four I would have gone over to the window and opened it putting it on the setting allowing the least air in or out. Then I'd get my cigarette and lighter while sitting on the window sill and leaning into the gap as much as possible to take my last nicotine fix for that day blowing the smoke out and glad we didn't have a house full of smoke alarms back then.

I went to sleep fairly quickly as I usually did on that bed, which has been my favourite bed of all time. This is because it comprised three very springy mattresses stacked on top of each other and so felt the way I imagine a water bed to feel but I don't know as I've never been lucky enough to try one. Some people may say what happened next was due to a horror story or an appalling news item seeping into my sub consciousness as I slept but the result was I woke up about three in the morning and I had an unflagging urge to get up, go and get a knife from the kitchen and find someone to try and kill them. I got up and got dressed into my jeans and denim shirt as it was early June so I was alright in that with my coat that I put on just before leaving the house. Having got dressed I went downstairs to the kitchen and opened the drawer with the serious knives, serving spoons and other culinary tools in. I took one which I didn't think would be missed too much as like in all kitchens we had favourites, knives used for only cutting bread and small ones who's handles were moulded to the shape of our hand. So finding one we didn't use a lot, I had a go at sharpening it with a tool that works by having the knife blade drawn through a narrow cleft in a sharpening stone fixed in a plastic holder. I then placed the blade which was about 10cm handle, 15cm cutting steel in my inside pocket as - being so long - it stuck out of all the other pockets and I wasn't about to leave the house with a handle protruding from my jacket. This was despite it being a pretty clear night and I didn't know where I was headed just looking to come across somebody and come out on them from behind a tree or round a corner with the aim of quickly cutting their throat and then leaving them to die. Whether of loss of blood or asphyxiation I didn't know or care I just left my home with the goal of returning to that place with having taken a life under my belt when I got back.

    I set off walking towards a local cemetery as that was one of the places I used to go and sit and think about 'life, the Universe and everything' Then, as I casually strolled through one of the more deprived areas of Plymouth with a large, sharpened carving knife poorly concealed in my jacket pocket at about three thirty in the morning of a day in June I wondered why I had an uncontrollable urge to kill the first person I came across. I felt as though I would kill anybody so I hoped it would be the sort of person that wouldn't give too much resistance.

Just as I approached the cemetery gates a police car pulled up from behind me and one of the two policemen wound down the window and leant out.

"Good morning Sir. You're out rather early aren't you?" He addressed me in a quite lackadaisical manner.

"I suppose so", I replied hoping to seem equally nonchalant.

"Are you going off to work or somewhere?" He questioned in a slightly more focussed style.

Still wishing to portray an unperturbed air I said, "Just out for a walk as I couldn't sleep Officer."

"Would you like a lift home?" the constable generously proffered.

"No thanks!" was my almost instantaneous reply, as I continued trying not to look agitated in the least.

"Well, it's time to head for home now anyway!" This was his most forceful remark.

"No problem!" My response was as off-handed as possible, yet I felt the lethal weapon shift in my pocket so the knife handle was millimetres from protruding from under my lapel.

The PC's radio gave a crackle and a message came through which attracted their attention much more than I did. I was wished a good night and the car headed off towards The Bluebird public house and other points of interest in

Higher Compton. Regardless of the instructions from the Devon and Cornwall Constabulary I proceeded towards the cemetery and the relentless droning of traffic rising up from The Parkway. I knew a way into the graveyard which could be used when the gates were locked and so I made my way through the gap between the end of the ancient stone wall and the start of the chain link fence as the two were not connected.

I progressed through the different areas of memorials to dead people, passing a section of headstones written in an Oriental script, a sizeable field of war graves, the Rose Garden and the mysterious Mausoleum. Then I came to the part of the burial ground which was being used, where I found graves; recently filled, about to be filled and halfway through being dug.

I think one reason I've always felt comfortable in a graveyard is that they are basically all pretty similar - domestic ones that is - as I feel that striding across an endless expanse of identical white war graves in Northern France or Arlington, and an unfortunately copious number of other sites, is an emotional overload. Particularly if one has personal links to it rather than just humanity. Another reason I'm 'at home' in a cemetery is that I've early memories of them. I don't really recall my mum's funeral service, but I do have a hazy recollection of a small box of ashes being put into the ground. Casting my mind back to when Dad and I still lived in the idyllic countryside village of Holt after the accident I can see him cutting the grass round the old church, tombs, and headstones. What I see clearest is the orange tint given to everything as the sun starts to set after a roasting hot midsummer day spent working hacking back the brambles and nettles with a scythe, then sickling away all the long grass between the graves, inside the rusty, flaking wrought iron fences of the family tombs and up against the wall of the church.

Back at the Plymouth graveyard I was at last on the opposite side to where I entered and there was a path down a slope towards an estate called 'Little America' due to the road names, e.g. Oregon Way, California Gardens and Nevada Close. I hadn't seen anyone except the policemen yet, but I hadn't expected to in the cemetery. I was now re-entering the real, inhabited streets which contained nothing but houses and homes which in turn were full of people. Not many out in the fresh air at around four in the morning of a weekday.

Further down the road I heard a front door slam shut. Somebody had just entered or left a house. I got up against a tree for cover and listened to see if I could hear any footfalls. Yes, I did and they were approaching me. It was a warm night, but I felt cold sweat on my palms, under my arms and trickling down my forehead. I leant back against the tree, gripping the knife in my right hand and covering that by pulling my jacket over with my left. The steps got closer and louder, but no faster as whomever it was continued up the hill towards me. An unrelated thought suddenly passed through my mind. The tree I was up against must have been there for years and I wondered if it had ever been witness to a murder before.

The innocent, unfortunate worker reached the tree and I slid round it to allow him to pass and then I could come up behind him. Time seemed to slow down for a few seconds and it was like I moved through transparent treacle, greatly restraining my freedom of movement. However I managed to get the knife over his right shoulder and up against his throat. Luckily with lightning fast reactions he grabbed my forearm and pushed it away from him so preventing the blade making a deep incision. He turned and fled back down the slope towards where he had come from. I dropped the knife and sprinted back up the hill to the cemetery. Slowing to more of a jogging pace I continued slowing till at the pace of a Sunday afternoon stroll I returned to the cul-de-sac which housed my home at its far end.

The sun was starting to rise on a day which would have immeasurably significant effects on the progress of the rest of my life. I entered the porch and then, as quietly as possible left my jacket on the coat rack, and returned to bed feeling guilt free at that moment and expecting my life to proceed unaltered when I woke up again at the usual time of about half seven.

When I woke up following the last good hours of sleep I would have for numerous days if not weeks except that which was tranquilizer induced I was suddenly hit by one thought.

"WHAT THE FUCKING HELL HAPPENNED LAST NIGHT!"

NO! THAT WASN'T A DREAM!!! I TRIED TO KILL SOMEONE LAST NIGHT!"

Talking to Dad was hard enough at the best of times. It was difficult to ask him if he wanted a cup of tea even when I was doing myself one. Usually I received a response such as, "Yes please. Do you want to get the biscuits and we can look at the next physics revision sheet over it?" I hated that, so did my best to keep myself to myself in my bedroom. So, if that was the case how could I go and say, "Good morning Dad! Have a good sleep last night? Me? Well not really. No. I just got up and tried to kill somebody I'd never met before."

It was impossible, but I had to say something to someone. I couldn't say anything to my school friends as I needed to speak pretty much immediately and as it was 1990 we didn't all have mobile phones. Hardly anyone in London had them, never mind the West Country where some farmers were still impressed by digital watches. Nobody in the family would be any good as it's not what one says to a great aunt by the phone as she makes her breakfast porridge for herself and Alsatian hound Sam.

My great friend S.P. was probably about top of the possibilities list but I didn't want to put such a weight on someone I knew had plenty of responsibility as it was and also suffered from clinical depression. We called it 'the black dog', as I understand Winston Churchill did. There was Reverend and Mrs Lovelace but they had two teenagers and a moderately deprived urban parish to care for so it wasn't fair to try them. Mind you, fairness had literally gone out the window years ago; yet through a windscreen in my case.

Then it occurred to me. I knew what I'd do. I'll call the people who always said they were there to talk to when that's what you needed. The Samaritans. Quite how, I'm not sure but if I recall correctly I asked Dad to stay in the kitchen so I could make a personal phone call in the living room. He agreed, I think seeing I was slightly out of order at the least and so presumed I was calling the doctor or such like. Years later I applied to join the Samaritans but I found that what I had talked to them about had provoked me to try and join them but prevented them from accepting me. Our conversation went something like this.

"...Good morning? My name's Annie...Do you want to talk to someone?"

"Well, not really, but I think I need to."

"O.K. would you like to give me your name? Or any name?"

"Alright Annie, I'm James."

"Anything especially you want to talk about, or just chat for company?"

"It's what happened last night."

"Right. Can you tell me what it was James?"

"Yeah Annie. I can tell you because you don't know who I am. My problem is I can't tell my dad."

"Dad, O.K. Are you a young man James? You don't sound too old."

"I'm just finishing school. 'A' levels. You know."

"So would you like to tell me about last night? Was it something you did or something that happened to you? Maybe something you saw or know about."

"Yes. I don't know why but I got up and tried to kill someone I'd never met before...Luckily I didn't hurt him too much...What should I do as I can't go and tell the police?"

So the conversation proceeded and Annie eventually persuaded me to grasp the dilemma by the horns, bite the bullet and tell my dad what had happened. His first response was to get the doctor out to have a talk to me. I think the GP provided him with a helping of moral support too as it was one he'd known for years. Obviously I don't know, but I imagine it must be quite distressing to get up on what seems an average morning and have your 'pride and joy' say they attempted murder for no reason during the night. I'm sure he had plans and ambitions for me at that stage of our relationship but I'm pretty sure having me as the first member of the family to go to court for attempted murder wasn't one of them.

As far as I can recall the GP felt he was somewhat out of his league despite having been doing the job for years. Mental health issues are always uncomfortable with most people except those who specialise in them. So what he did was arrange for me to go to the Seven Trees clinic and meet a mental health social worker and a psychiatrist. I don't know why, but clinics which deal with neurotics and psychotics have names which are euphemistic. Seven Trees, Moorhaven, Glenbourne and in the extreme case Broadmoor. If you didn't know what that was you'd imagine it was a class hotel out in the Yorkshire moors, not the home of many of the most dangerous men in the country. I had only turned eighteen a few weeks before but that meant I was old enough to face this NHS interrogation panel by myself, despite the fact I felt like I was in a dream/nightmare and wasn't sure if it was real or if I'd wake up in a few minutes to find I had a face full of cat whiskers which often woke me up back in those days.

They gave me a good quizzing and then left me in my dad's company having a social services cup of tea, which I became acclimatised to over the following weeks. They came back and told me they had concluded that I needed to be sectioned. Being naive at the age of eighteen I hadn't heard of Sectioning under the Mental Health Act until I suddenly found it was happening to me. The following events are a bit of a muddle, and the ones so far aren't exactly crystal clear, but I know that the day I got up and told my dad I'd tried to kill someone that night I found myself in Moorhaven around teatime, being kept there by the Mental Health Act as there was fear I'd be a danger to myself or other members of society.

The next big question was how the police discovered about me as I talked to the various medical professionals knowing they were restrained by confidentiality laws and so they couldn't tell anybody else. I don't recall taking a decision to inform the police, for as far as I could tell there was no way this crime could be linked to me. I didn't know who the unfortunate Royal Mail worker was that I met in Little America and he had no way to identify me. I think I had dropped the carving knife and it was then found by the detectives investigating the scene of the crime. Yet, I wasn't on their database then so despite my fingerprints being all over the handle there would be no match.

People regularly say 'Honesty is the best policy' but if I hadn't been honest I don't think I would have been picked up and charged with attempted murder as they wouldn't have known a thing about me. Yet I do remember being interviewed by a couple of police officers and the conversation being taped while I was at the psychiatric unit.

I remember at the time I was still rather confused about what was going on, what I had done, and I was taking my epilepsy drugs with a few tranquilisers that reduced my brain function and mental dexterity. 'Liquid cosh' was the standard nickname used by both staff and clients for the substance we all received as standard practice. We were supposed to call ourselves clients yet we said victims or inmates much to the annoyance of the nurses and matrons. If one wasn't treated with the liquid cosh back in those days you might well have got Electroconvulsive Therapy. I know that was used to treat really bad cases of clinical depression as one of the guys I managed to have a sensible conversation with in there was receiving such. It certainly seemed to be quite effective as when he arrived on our ward he didn't feel like moving a muscle yet after a few weeks of ECT he had the energy and motivation to get up and get himself to a green on the local golf course while still in his pyjamas. I remember there was a girl on the same ward as the two of us and it was very difficult to understand what she was trying to say to us as she was suffering from a heavy dose of liquid cosh for sure. She had been given that due to her acute psychosis, schizophrenia, paranoia or neurosis. It probably wasn't the case but it seemed to me and a couple of the other more comprehensible inmates that she believed the packet of Polo mints she had in her hand was a train with each mint being a separate carriage and her mouth being a tunnel the train had to go into.

I stayed in the Moorhaven psychiatric unit for about five weeks at the end of which I went to Plymouth magistrate's court only really expecting to have to confirm my name and address. I'm not sure but I think Moorhaven was considered a secure unit as I remember I wasn't allowed out in the grounds by myself but I could take escorted walks with members of staff or visitors. I received numerous calls from members of my family and good family friends such as the Lovelace's. They were a family that replaced S.P. and her family when they moved up country. Very similar as it was composed of two intelligent adults with the principal breadwinner employed in a very professional activity. With S.P. her husband had been a member of the navy and with the Lovelace's he was a member of the Church of England priesthood. John was a caring, sincere vicar who built up quality relationships with children including his own two teenage sons and with local adults in a deprived area of urban Plymouth regardless of their faith or beliefs and uninfluenced by their history. He had an enterprising wife who needed to find a way to occupy time, having got her two children Mike and Phil into secondary school and finding they were ready to take on a bit more freedom and thus begin learning by making their own mistakes. They weren't the type of teenagers to be mummy's boys and she'd not have allowed them to be clingy anyway.

She went on to start a small business which sold non-alcoholic wines and beers. Unfortunately it never took off as this was in the late eighties before we had a national reputation for binge drinking and before anybody had heard of the World Wide Web, eBay and PayPal as I think these would have helped with the marketing side of the commercial enterprise.

Mike was a pupil in the year below me in Plymouth Grammar School and was a talented musician. He played bass guitar for a band called Die Laughing who appeared to be about as meek and mild as Lemmy from Motorhead after a week of sleepless nights. They played at the Cooperage, supporting bands who visited while on the South West leg of their national tours; people following bands such as Hellbastard, Bolt Thrower, Lawnmower Deth and Filthy Christians. I familiarised myself with these musical artists by obtaining compilation albums from the record label most of them used which was called Earache. I was always more and more amazed as I got to know Mike and another member of Die Laughing who was a member of my biology class. He wasn't a close friend but I was quite happy to dissect a rat with him on a Monday morning or set up an experiment involving osmosis to be checked at the end of the week. The incredible thing was that these were guys who I could talk to about my pussycat "Brum" and seriously discuss emotional, touchy feely thoughts regarding relationships with. Yet in the blink of an eye they transformed into demonically possessed children of Satan and took on names such as Schizophrenic Rotary Spinmaster, who was a guitarist with Lawnmower Deth; one of my favourite bands of the era. To such an extent I got two of their CDs and a sweatshirt sent by post from Nottingham.

Things which don't quite follow the line or are slightly off kilter have often been the ones to appeal to me and this was when my music tastes really took off on a tangent to run of the mill. I liked people who challenged the expectations, norms and mores of the surrounding cultural ocean, rising up out of it like a volcano off the coast of Iceland or Hawaii. If people managed to produce an album with song titles such as "Seventh church of the Apocalyptic Lawnmower" and "Satan's Trampoline" I'll confess they had my attention.

Slowly but surely we evolved and Mike joined a band called Largeman which included a noticeably talented song writer called Simon and so led to everyone in the group moving to Stoke Newington and having a go at making it in the big time. The whole concept of 'Us and Them', celebrities and humans, famous and real people was very different back in the early nineties. That was when we started to drift apart and he developed a taste for family life.

Chapter 12

Meanwhile I had been transported into the Hospital Wing of HMP Exeter from Moorhaven, the number one 'mad house' in Devon, if not the whole West Country which had seemed very Victorian in a number of ways. Despite being a young offender, I went to the Hospital Wing rather the YOs unit for a couple of reasons. Firstly I was epileptic and till they knew to what degree it was sensible to keep me near the medical facilities. Also the prison officers knew I'd been charged with 'attempted murder' due to a mental breakdown so it seemed a good idea and it was less crowded. HMP Exeter is terrible for overpopulation nowadays and wasn't much different then. I'm sure there was at least one suicide while I stayed.

I don't know how many victims one must accumulate to be a serial killer or a mass murderer but it was then I came closest to knowingly meeting one. There was a quiet, reclusive, subdued gent apparently from Exeter Uni's literati in the cell next door and we chatted to pass the time. Talking to somebody you can't see was a familiar experience due to telephones but I found it strange being in a room next to somebody and talking to them by raising my voice while stood either at the barred widow or by the door. Back then prison was a distressingly unpleasant experience without each of the cells containing TVs and more beverage facilities than most public libraries, like a very rough edged Premier

Inn, as it is these days. These days I know people who think about committing a crime aiming to get sent to prison so they will be guaranteed a roof over their head, three meals a day and also to be off the streets at Christmas. The trouble is what you have to do to be sure of being sent down. Unless you're a murderer, rapist, top drug dealer and maybe an arsonist you'll probably be out again before you know it, especially if it was your first offence. I am really horrified by the sentences handed out by judges these days. I watched a Channel Four documentary series about Human Traffickers who smuggled young women over from Eastern Europe and then set them up in brothels. I was particularly concerned when they said one of them was in Plymouth so I for all I knew I could have passed these criminals in the street and could have chatted with them in a local bar. What I found really distressing was that when the Organised Crime Unit nicked all the perpetrators none of them got more than four years. I was thinking and hoping they would be getting nearer fourteen years for establishing sites for what was basically financially motivated rape.

Getting back to my cell neighbour from Exeter Uni; we didn't ask each other what we'd done to get where we were as it's not the done thing, as one is told in *The Shawshank Redemption*. Although when he was off talking to the prison psychiatrist other inmates carrying out deliveries, cleaning or locked up within shouting distance said he had been Mr Normal himself till he came home early one afternoon and found his wife of a lengthy period in bed with somebody. He had been quiet by nature so he made his discovery without being noticed himself. So he went back down stairs and out to the shed with its petrol driven mower and a refill can. He locked the house shut from the outside and then poured all the petrol through the letterbox and followed it with a match. I don't think he did much to resist arrest and indeed may have still been at the house when the emergency services arrived or handed himself in to a police station shortly after having been out for his last good meal and a drink for a considerable length of time in his favourite local restaurant.

Becoming a resident of HMP Exeter had a strong influence on what I read for a while as it provoked me into reading Oscar Wilde's fantastic "Ballad of Reading Gaol" which I doubt I'd have discovered till much later otherwise. Once the health workers had assessed my level of threat to myself and others and concluded I didn't need to be worried about I was moved into a shared young offenders cell from my individual hospital cell. I had to be escorted from one side of the prison to the other twice a day to receive my epilepsy medication from the Hospital Wing. At home it had been in tablet form but here it was liquid so I couldn't hide it under my tongue and then sell it on the prison black market as a tranquiliser. I remember I regularly walked past a curious architectural outcrop which couldn't be seen from outside the walls while going to and from medication. It had windows on two levels with a narrow separation by a floor between them. It was clear that this floor contained a trapdoor and via these windows hangings could be witnessed with the convict being aligned with the top window and then falling through the floor to be suspended a few feet above the lower floor and so visible through the bottom window. I think seeing this brought home to me the intensity of Oscar Wilde's verses.

When I was on remand in Exeter, at first I had been quite worried about being bullied and victimised in protection rackets by inmates who were more familiar with life behind bars than I was. I got the impression some people saw life behind bars as a second home and it didn't matter which prison in the country they were residing in as being 'institutionalised' it was just the repetitive timetable of each day which they were paying attention to. Fortunately as I was recognised as being 'a psycho', most people did all they could to avoid me, not knowing how I would react to any abuse. Once this became clear I occupied myself by developing a cold, emotionless, glazed stare a member of *Carcharodon carcharias* would have been proud of. Yes, that's a Great White Shark. I'd never been a skilled small talker and chatting with a cell mate required a few skills and some knowledge I had yet to obtain. For example there is a specific language of prison slang and acronyms which I was unaware of, e.g. D and D - a few weeks before had meant the role playing game Dungeons and Dragons to me, but was now Drunk and Disorderly. Then most youths had a number of TDA convictions, or TWOCs as it is now, due to fine tuning adjustments to the law. Take and Drive Away or Take With Out Consent.

My shark stare obviously worked as one time when we were out in the exercise yard I overheard two partners in crime discussing cellmates.

"You're in with that new schizo guy from Plymouth aren't you?" said Slasher.

"Yeah. I don't trust him so I've hardly had a moment's kip since he got in!" replied 642 angrily.

642 was a Welsh boyo. Many of the lads with Welsh accents had numbers for names and at first I couldn't understand it. Then I remembered the significant piece of English cinematic history 'Zulu' which was Michael Caine's first performance. In that there are so many Joneses and Evans' that the last few digits of their military number or prison number in this case became a name.

"You poor sod! The Scouser I'm in with is OK as far as they ever are. He likes his dope and he's getting it in on his visits. We play cards for burn and he gives us a spliff or two to keep things chilled out. Can't ask for more really," smirked Slasher.

"If you get me a bit of puff I'll sort you out a few straights at canteen. On Wednesday isn't it?" replied 642 looked as if he was falling asleep in the yard, trying to use this sixty minutes for sleep rather than exercise. It was a real suntrap as it had high walls on every side, some to other parts of the prison and one to the real world. Not that I knew it then, but it made sense of the lines Wilde repeats in his classic poem.

I never saw a man who looked
With such a wistful eye
Upon that little tent of blue
Which prisoners call the sky.

Not that many people engaged me in conversation but on the few occasions they did one favourite thing to do was wind me up by saying that due to me being crazy I'd get an At Her Majesty's Pleasure sentence at Broadmoor so it was dependant on my behaviour if or when I would ever be released.

One thing which stuck in my mind from the Young Offenders Wing of HMP Exeter which was a very familiar thing there but not something I encountered in any of the psychiatric units I went to before or after was 'a padded cell'. In the prison it was called the strip cell, as you would be stripped before being thrown in it. This was to prevent you using shoe laces or anything to make a noose or suchlike. As inmates who were put in there were usually absolute furiously angry about something the screws had just done, be it discover their stashed drugs or found that they were the ones who had just PP9ed somebody. PP9ing was the name given to taking a couple of batteries, or ideally a big brick like battery such as a PP9 and putting it in a sock to make an improvised mace which was a very good weapon with which to have a go at a 'nonce' or a 'grass'. People who were kept separate from the main body of prisoners due to being sex offenders, paedophiles or rapists were the ones governed by Rule 43 which meant they had to have their meals by themselves in their cells and they never had exercise or association with ones who weren't under Rule 43. These were the ones called the 'nonces' and once you acquired this label you would never get rid of it, so it was a weapon used to blackmail the 'new boys' into giving up everything they had and in the worst occasions even more than that. I remember one time in Exeter a couple of Scousers blackmailed a lad by threatening to spread rumours about him being a 'nonce' unless he gave them the address of one of his best mates. What they wanted to do was have a contact of theirs on the outside send parcels of cannabis to that address and then get the victim's mate to smuggle it in at a visit. So they would be having drugs delivered without having to do any of it themselves.

If they had been caught with drugs they probably would have had a stint in the strip cell before being taken to E Wing, the punishment block. What they often did to let off some of their steam in the strip cell was shout abuse for hours and wipe their urine and faeces all over the walls and their bodies.

The confession for this chapter is one I'm particularly unhappy about. In the remand centre inmates frequently and rapidly came and went so few people had any mates as there was hardly time to get know anyone before they were out on bail, released or sent down and so evacuated to the Young Offenders Institute nearest their home. However, unfortunately being held for a serious accusation I was going to be on remand for a serious length of time; five months in total. Thus I was put in a slightly bigger cell than average with a guy called Parker who was familiar with the experience, and was not the kind of guy I would like to meet in a dark alley even if I was supported by a SWAT team. For the first week or two he kept his distance but I hadn't spent 200 million years evolving my heartless stare as the sharks had so eventually he saw through my front. To start with I was just subtly cooperative, letting him win at cards and keeping him supplied with 'burns'. It soon became clear he had been a womaniser when free as previous girlfriends he had ripped off or those who had done it to him were a principal subject of conversation. He also decorated the cell walls with every Sun page three he could get hold of. Somehow he obtained a copy of a top shelf magazine which led to an embarrassing incident one day. I had been taken from the cell for some reason but was returned to it earlier than he had expected as the door was quickly unlocked, I entered and was locked in. For a second I thought I had it to myself for a short time but then I realised he had been in the corner behind the door masturbating over his Razzle. I couldn't have timed it worse as he was just at the point of no return when I interrupted. He was furious but too drained to indulge in violence so just gave me an extensive example of verbal abuse. That was not enough to satisfy him so that night after 'lights out' I confess I was blackmailed into giving him a massage. Luckily he was homophobic so didn't make me go below his waistline but apparently such things often happened in some cells and even more intimate relationships were indulged in while showering. Sometimes involving consent but not always. Another time he tried to get a rub-down from me but by then I was so fed up with his company I resisted, probably thinking that a black eye or similar was an acceptable price to get myself a different cellmate. Knowing he would be punished for such blatant brutality he instead chose to hold me down and shave my eyebrows off for me. If you have light hair and a pale face it not so bad but with thick dark hair such as mine the absence of a line of hair below your forehead looks quite ridiculous.

I never got caught with anything I shouldn't have had, but that's not because I never had it. So I never went to the punishment wing. I think the worst cells I ever spent any length of time were those under Bristol Crown Court which are really dungeons. I wouldn't have been surprised if in that dark, dingy subterranean complex they had an oubliette or two. As there was at Exeter prison they probably had facilities for execution somewhere and considering how ancient it all was I reckon Tony Robinson and the Time Team could have a field day there. I'm sure if I'd been able to look at the walls with a bit more light I'd have found graffiti from the age when Bristol was involved in the slave trade and probably tried smugglers in the court rooms. The other particularly unpleasant cells which most people spend at least a little time in are those in the back of the police meat wagons which take inmates to and fro between police stations, courtrooms and prisons. Then they were divided into cells so small that if you're tall and have long legs it's too tight for you to sit down. It gave me a bit of an idea what it's like to be an industrially farmed chicken. Those vans are the ones with tiny windows like square portholes that you see the paparazzi photographers hold cameras up to when the latest serial killer is being taken from The Old Bailey. I had a few trips in one of those which each lasted a few hours going between Plymouth, Exeter, Bristol and Portland. I think the worst of the lot was when one day I was on remand in Exeter and was suddenly told to pack up and get ready to move as I was going up to Portland. I knew it would happen sometime but it wasn't meant to be till after I was convicted. However, Exeter was so overcrowded I was moved up to Portland as a remand prisoner which wasn't what that institution was meant for. That was bad enough but to really give me an emotional kick in the balls they chose to do it on a visit day so just as I was going out of the gate at Exeter I saw my dad in a queue to get into the visit centre. There was no way I could tell anyone for hours till we got in at Portland but by then he knew that he would have to drive up to Dorset to see me which he frequently did and I'm indescribably grateful for.

Chapter 13

When I first received an empty diary at Portland with a page of A5 for each day I was a bit doubtful that enough would happen for me to be able to fill a page a day but that soon turned out to be the least of my problems. Like most diaries these days it had tables of conversion charts, world standard times and notable dates in the first few pages. After that my dad had written in all the names and addresses he thought I could possibly want or need. In the back were pages for organising financial incomings and outgoings but not being like Harry 'Grouty' in Porridge these were no use to me.

Rather than write this part of my book in diary style like Ann Frank, Adrian Mole or Samuel Pepys I've decided to sift through and pluck out some of the more interesting or amusing elements and quote directly if I find some of the passages stand out. I'll start with the first paragraph of the whole document, word for word.

"The diary of J.G. Bridgwater VL1787. I am a convicted prisoner at Portland Young Offenders Institution at the present, having been sentenced to three years for 'Attempted malicious wounding with intent to cause grievous bodily harm.' I've yet to find anybody with a longer winded impressive sounding charge than that."

On New Year's Day we had three sessions of association, which was when we got to watch TV, play snooker and enjoy each other's company as much as that was possible. This was particularly difficult in the TV room. Any film which lacked mass destruction or gratuitous violence was received with exclamations of "Boring! Dull! Too intellectual!" What was more trying than anything else was the hypocritical way the other inmates behaved. Half the time they were complaining about people talking over the TV and the other half they leant over to the person next to them and told them what was about to happen in the film.

I had stayed up the night before to see in the New Year which was greeted by much shouting, whistling and foghorns from down in Portland harbour, which still had navy activity in those days. I think it must have been about the bleakest New Year I've ever seen in as at the time I thought I'd be inside till past the next New Year. However in fact I got parole and so was released on December 5th of the year just beginning which was 1991. I did a total of eighteen months locked up including remand. I had been listening to Radio 4 at midnight and was disappointed they didn't play 'Auld Lang Syne' after Big Ben struck the hour. I thought they would be traditionalist enough to do that but no. My biggest concern at the time was the wind blowing through the gaps of my window frame. It was usually OK but that night a force nine gale was howling round 'Colditz for kids' as some people called it. Already being very keen on literature I smiled to myself when I had heard someone on the radio ask; "Is J.R.R. Tolkien Hobbit forming?" When in detention I found little things like that could do a lot to cheer me up and, as I realised more and more as time went, by small things could make a big difference. For example if I got two sausages rather than one for breakfast that made the difference between an average and a good day.

If I hadn't had my radio/personal stereo I do wonder what my sanity would have done. That kept me in touch with the real world and visits and letters were like brilliant rays of light from a lighthouse searing through an indescribably dark sky. I remember listening to John Cleese talking to his shrink on Radio 4 about their book *"Families and how to survive them."* If possible I'd listen next week as then the subject was Fathers, a topic very close to my heart.

All of us who had just arrived at the induction house of Hardy in the last few days received a talk from the Senior Probation Officer in an afternoon. To start I thought she must have one of the worst jobs in the whole place as she lacked a prison officer's disciplinary power. Thus she got heckled at almost every sentence she spoke and nobody heckles harder than a bunch of foolish, inattentive teenage convicts who think they know it all. Also they have attitude problems beyond belief as whenever they are challenged by the surrounding authorities for misbehaving, their run of the mill answer is, "Well, what are you going to do about it? Send me to prison? Ha! Nice idea!" The tiresome taunters got their comeuppance at the end of it all however as she said with a smile at the end of the session that she'd see each of us one to one and then write reports to hand on to the Parole Board. I can't think when I've seen so many faces drop simultaneously in unison.

In what felt like an attempt to compensate for paying such minimal attention to maintaining my personal trimming I found myself in an establishment where I was obliged to remove all the facial hair I could with a single blade disposable razor and to use the same blade for a week. Then once a week I had to hand in the now edgeless blade, showing the duty Prison Officer it was still in position within its plastic casing and had not been removed to supply me with a piece of cutting equipment. Depending on what one was intending to cut one could take the blade if one got hold of one by one means or another and possibly attach it to a handle. The legendary trick on this front was to snap the blade in half and then by softening the plastic handle of a toothbrush with a flame each half could be secured on a separate side of the handle. This then provided two blades with a gap of a few millimetres between them, which if used to give a 'slashing' would be particularly hard to stitch up again and would leave a very visible scar for the remaining life.

Blades weren't required just for enhancing acts of violence though. My favourite use of a razor blade was linked to my nicotine addiction as I often found I had numerous Rizlas, enough baccy to make a slim 'burn'; especially if I had sacrificed quality for quantity at that week's canteen and so had a pouch of Clan pipe tobacco rather than ½ a packet of Golden Virginia rolling baccy and a couple of Red Band tailor made straights which were sold individually. The infuriating problem was to have all those and be out of matches. Then however I discovered that with a steady hand and a good blade a match could be quartered so providing four times as many ignitions from a single box of matches.

There were other little tricks like that which I had quickly picked up in the Young Offenders wing of HMP Exeter. Things such as using porridge as glue to stick pictures on the cell walls, and when your AA Duracell batteries run out for your personal stereo or radio the thing to do was to bash them about a bit, leave them on a radiator and if neither of those are practical just chew it for a while and it was surprising how much more energy could be obtained. Some of the tricks are specific to the environment and so had to be learnt on site at Portland. Also they were more specific than that as some of them depended on which wing you were in. The oldest parts of the prison, which were the standard shape and layout of a big open space in the middle with walkways along the side walls, off which came the cells wasn't the structure of the entire place. In addition there were 'Rodney' and 'Hardy' which were much newer buildings shaped like 'Y' as there were three wings off the hub containing the office where the various Prison Officers sat around and drank tea while watching the CCTV and smoking. Everyone went through 'Hardy' as it was the training house in which it was compulsory to spend a number of weeks so as to learn the prison routine and schedule with discipline added in too. Having come from a well-disciplined secondary school I didn't have a problem addressing the staff with titles such as 'Sir', 'Boss' or once they permitted it 'Mr Whoever'.

The greatest initial pleasure about Portland, which applied to Hardy and then Nelson when I was moved there was having a cell to myself. Nelson had a reputation for housing 'baby burglars' so why I was put there I don't know. If I remember it was the nearest to the medical department which could well have been the reason, as twice a day I had to go and get my epilepsy medication. There certainly were 'baby burglars' in there as I got to know one lad called Marcus from Bristol area who was a 'creeper' by trade. This meant he broke in a house in the early morning, hopefully knowing the floor plan somehow and so tip-toed around picking up car keys, wallets, passports and, with particular victims, picking up their drugs stash too. Dealers obviously couldn't phone the cops next morning saying they had been robbed of a few kilos of coke and a replica handgun. I think Marcus was just seventeen having been caught as a sixteen year old with a record an arm's length already and so got a custodial sentence. He claimed to feel guilty about freaking out some women he had known and robbed. Apparently and understandably they were horrified waking to find they been visited that night in the bedroom as well as the rest of the house.

One day I remember hadn't been too bad a day as I was late for supper as was often the case due to my having to go to the medical department for my epilepsy medication at suppertime. Every day I needed to go and pick up my medication so my epilepsy was not a problem. One thing I never understood was how something like that can be so routine it happened every day like clockwork but then once in a blue moon it failed to happen and so due to missing it or having my medication significantly late I would occasionally have a fit. When I did have a fit it was always in my cell by myself and it was very confusing. One time particularly as I recovered consciousness after a fit I thought it was bedtime and so made my bed up and started getting undressed. Then the duty screw came in and I found he was expecting me to be ready to go off to parade as it was actually the start of the day and I had just got up. Being confused following my fit I mistook seven in the morning for seven in the evening.

I am glad I had to go and collect my medicine daily though as it often meant I was late to pick up supper. That meant if there was any food left over I often got it and so sometimes had three sausages rather than just one. It's surprising how much difference a few grams of shrivelled pork can make when you're in certain physical and mental conditions. Also I heard a great line on the radio, "Despite popular belief, cubism is not a load of balls." I would have missed hearing that if I got my supper with everyone else.

I'm usually very patient but I got quite angry and frustrated waiting for a psychiatrist who was supposed to see me one morning. He would have been the fifth one I had seen since the whole episode began. I never got the impression any of them had any answers for me and I definitely didn't feel I understood what had happened and why. I was never convinced they knew why either. Fortunately the 'trick cyclist' turned up after lunch and saved me from a lengthy exercise in self-control as I hadn't used the proper toilet during the last 'slop out' and if I hadn't gone to the medical wing I'd have had to control my bowels for almost four hours or use the 'slop pot.' While out visiting the doctor, I was told by someone I looked like a Catholic. This seemed a very curious statement and I've often wondered about it since and wondered if the Pope looks like a Catholic. I've got friends who have either gone to or from Catholicism and I wondered if while doing so their appearance changed. Being a devout

Catholic is probably a good thing while inside so as to discourage suicide, as according to rumours there had just been one success and one failed suicide attempted that week.

Every morning our cells were given a quick inspection and Saturday morning was the Governor's Inspection which was a much more intense, detailed check. The mood or temperament of the inspecting officer was clearly very significant in such things as I was failed and given a re-scrub one day due to having left some rubbish in my dustpan. I assumed the screw didn't 'get his end away' the night before and so was in a foul temper as plenty of times before I had passed when I still had trash in my pan but not that time. It was also kit change that day which was when we all handed in our week old disposable razors and got new ones as long as the blade was still in the one being handed in.

I confess I probably let my personal hygiene go a bit while inside due to the difficulty in maintaining standards. For example I tried to have a shower during association but it really was a struggle against the odds. The first problem being there's no temperature control so you had to pop under the scalding downpour for a second and then duck out to spend a few seconds returning to a bearable temperature and try and do some cleaning before getting a chill due to the freezing cold air filling the room. Then after that ordeal one had to try and dry with a towel very reminiscent of a flannel due to its size and texture.

Chapter 14

A force ten gale blew through the gaps around my window and made a very irritating whistling sound so I had to turn up my radio when listening to a very interesting 'Science Now' program which came from the British Psychological Society's Annual Conference. I got a couple of uplifting rays of light spiritually speaking via postage; one from Dad saying our friends the Lovelaces had decided to give him their brown Burmese cat Rags as she doesn't get on with their Boxer dog Impy, short for Impedimenta who was the wife of Vitalstatistix in the Asterix cartoon books.

I recall when I had PE for the first time in about a month as we didn't have it in Exeter and it nearly killed me. We did team competitions over a range of circuit training routines, often involving medicine balls. I don't remember ever having felt so close to passing out and despite my legs feeling like jelly, my vision blurring and not being able to think straight, I impressed myself with my will power. I dread to think what would have happened if I'd failed; probably a short trip to E wing, the punishment block.

I remember when I met Mrs C., the Head of the Education Department for the first time. She had the job of giving me and all the other new inmates a brief sexual education. She showed us a prison service video about AIDS and HIV+ which pulled no punches due to the audience it was designed for. I certainly got the impression from some of the screws there that some inmates are treated similarly to Pavlov's dogs. After the film we were then given a display of condoms by Mrs C. In total she had about fifty of different colours, flavours and textures. I couldn't help wondering how the people at the local chemist viewed her, as condom collecting would have appeared to be her hobby and she was sixty five if she was a day old.

Some lads came up from Exeter and I saw it was faces I recognised but I didn't have a chance to have a chat immediately. Half of them got put straight into the main wings rather than the induction wing because things were so crowded there as all the prisons in this country were and still are. As we were told the recidivism rate was 70% they were probably familiar, if not comfortable, with prison life and routine. As I was getting to know my neighbours I began feeling sorry for them and glad I'd achieved what I had during my childhood. For example it was distressing finding how many of them couldn't read and write. I hardly knew these guys but I'd already been asked then bribed to read and write very intimate letters for people. How one avoids insanity if one can't lose oneself in a book in that type of place beats me. I didn't expect these guys to read what I did but I'm sure they'd have liked Stephen King, the Krays life story and *The Godfather* etc. At that time I was reading *Scoop* by Evelyn Waugh and by the time I'd left there I'd have read a couple of books I liked so much I had to get them for my dad. The ones which really got to me were *Zen and the Art of Motorcycle Maintenance* by Robert Pirsig and *Deep Time* by David Darling. I was so captured by the title of Mr Pirsig's book that I had to pick it up and read it. I was so glad I did as now it's one of my favourite pieces of literature and I've given copies to my dad and a good friend who has now gone on to be a Street Pastor. *Deep Time* is what I consider a clever book as it works like this. It starts at the birth of the universe with a gold atom which is formed.

It then follows the atom through the whole of time to where it becomes involved in very sophisticated computer circuitry and if I remember right it gets put in the 'Voyager' satellite and sent out into deep space. These were both books I was surprised to find in the YOI's library. I suppose a lot of the books they had there were ones left behind when people were released.

When I got moved to my cell in Nelson it was a revelation. The cell had windows I could open which had bars outside them. They had wet rot and when it started raining they let in floods so I was building up a personal water supply just below the heating pipe which ran along by the wall under the window. There was also a freezing draught coming in which meant even if I went to bed wearing both my tee-shirts and my sweatshirt it still made me think of Scott of the Antarctic who was born just up the road from where I live in Plymouth. The blankets were very reminiscent of fine fishing nets with some strands missing as if whenever anyone wanted some string they just extracted a thread from a blanket. Fortunately Nelson, like the other main houses/wings, was structured the way I expected prisons to be having seen them from the outside at Dartmoor and inside in films like Porridge and McVicar. If it hadn't been I think I'd have felt cheated as if I went to prison I obviously wanted to do it properly.

I had another talk with Mrs C. in which I tried to persuade her to take me on to the full-time education detail. She was Scottish and very straight talking. There were also a lot of Welsh inmates in Portland at the time and I began to feel that being Celtic and being direct may well be correlated. Another murderous exercise session followed lunch on that day. Being out in the open in rough weather was bad enough when I was fully dressed and torment being out in shorts and a vest. By the time I'd done 240 exercises such as press ups, sit ups, squats and 48 lengths of a five-a-side pitch carrying a medicine ball of 70kg I couldn't think when I'd ever been so exhausted.

There were quite a few Bristolians in at the time as the riots at Pucklechurch had taken place just a few months before. Rob and Andy were a couple of guys from Bristol I got to know fairly well in the education department. They had been doing armed robberies of Post Offices comparatively well until a slight lack of attention let them down. Probably a case of familiarity breeding contempt as for a while things seemed to go too well. They had been cutting phone lines first then going in so the unfortunate sub-Post Office keepers couldn't alarm anyone till the robbers were well away. However one time they cut the wrong lines and so the police were on their tail too quick for an escape. They had the sense to use their time inside to work on their literacy and numeracy as it's called now, just Maths and English as we called it then. Some inmates didn't like my public school way of speaking or didn't like the fact I had nine GCSE's and was doing 'A' levels with the aim of going to university. I reckon those two had dealt with public school kids in Bristol selling hash and coke for their posh parties and so weren't put off by me saying I came from Bath and not pronouncing it like Americans say Math. They called me 'Dictionary Breath' or 'Professor' and got me to help them doing fractions. Some guys got me to write or read letters for them once those two had told them I was alright despite talking like the Royalty.

As I had got a three year sentence once I made a pleading deal, going guilty to malicious wounding with intent rather than going to trial in Crown Court for attempted murder, I had to find a way to pass the time. I was still planning to go to university eventually so I decided to resume my 'A' level work. Thanks to my very kind chemistry teacher who was also my tutor at Plymouth College it was arranged so I could do the course by correspondence. He organised everything so I could receive worksheets and mock papers in biology and chemistry and then when we reached the exam season I did some special extra papers instead of actually doing practical tests. I got B in the chemistry and got a D in biology. What I didn't realise at the time was that Mr Hobbs did it for me because he was a Christian and so a great believer in charity and for no other reason.

One night's film restored my morale as it was "Cobra" with Sylvester Stallone. I must admit I prefer 'Sylvester, the puddy-tat' and 'Daffy Duck' is my favourite Disney character. We often past the time by discussing which the better one was and debated what would happen if certain superheroes and villains took each other on in combat. For example, who would win in a fight between Incredible Hulk and Superman?

I remember I had a visit from Dad with my uncle and aunt, the Archers, one afternoon. It was good in as much as I received my music tapes and some textbooks so I could get on with my 'A' level chemistry and biology. However what didn't impress me was that it seemed they were using it as a chance to catch up with each other, telling Christmas/New Year stories as they didn't see each other more than about twice a year normally in those days. I got back to my cell and found the floor was saturated by the rain during the visit. I had just enough battery power to listen to my favourite four songs and then had to go on to the radio. I got the last from the AA batteries by giving them a beating to last long enough to get through to next association and so make a deal to get some more batteries.

If anyone had been thinking they were having a rough time there at Portland I think they'd have had a rethink after watching a particular film. One night we had 'Papillon' with Dustin Hoffman and Steve McQueen. I hadn't been to the 'block' and I intended to keep things that way as I had heard some frightening stories. However I didn't think it would involve being locked in a blackened room for a couple of months with nothing but bread and water with cockroaches for company. However I knew we did have the same insect companions as they did as I had come across cockroach racing in Exeter. They were also kept as pets by some inmates as they fitted neatly in a matchbox.

I don't know what caused it but I must confess one evening I had a really bad attack of homesickness and melancholy. If my personality from prep school days had seen me then I'd have been appalled. I reckon it was due to listening to music which I'd last heard when I was out in the real free world enjoying life and it brought back lots of happy but now distant memories. Usually the seagulls there were just an annoying choir of cacophonous irritants which just annoyed screws and cons alike. However I had to laugh at one of the birds as I saw it trying to drink out of a frozen puddle. It was having no success and just slipped about looking more and more foolish and frustrated. It made me think it was a metaphor for the effect of the prison system. As we were often told the recidivism rate was about 70% and by the time I'd finished my sentence there some people will have come in, done their time, been released and then come back in again. It's when I think on lines like that it all seems so pointless and unproductive, regardless of the amount of effort applied, like the seagull's attempt at getting a drink.

To help pass the time I decided to do a Computer Literacy and Information Technology course. I was familiar with ZX Spectrums as I had one myself and Dad had a BBC machine. The one we worked on inside was an Acorn with an Archimedes program which, not that I knew it then, would be replaced by Microsoft Office as it had word processing, spread sheets and databases. Back then nobody had an idea what a PowerPoint presentation was as it was unheard of. While in the education block courtyard having a smoke I bumped into Barnes who I had known while on remand in Exeter. I couldn't say why but I got the impression he was pretending to be OK but I felt it was a false front and that it was all really getting to him. It was surprising what being involved with something you're familiar with and recognise can do to calm stressed nerves. It would have been around then I met up with my old friends from 'A' level chemistry again, such as molarity, ionisation energy and entropy and I enjoyed their company more than I ever had before.

I was very disappointed by someone I talked to as they asked where I came from and they didn't know where Plymouth was and weren't any better educated when I said it was past Exeter and they didn't know where that was either. There were some seriously unenlightened souls in the establishment on both sides of the doors. I knew I'd been well educated and was well read but I hadn't expected to find myself thinking on those lines when I met my probation officer. She came up to see me for the first time and while we were chatting I found out she didn't know who Evelyn Waugh was. I didn't expect her to necessarily have read any but at least know who I was talking about.

Chapter 15

Some people seemed to thrive on violence and intimidation but the more sensible individuals usually manage to avoid it. However I remember when I had someone I didn't know approach me and say he'd rearrange my face for me if I didn't give him a half ounce of baccy which I owed him. I didn't know if he'd just mistaken my identity or thought I looked an easy target. I had to deal with it myself as there were two things it was fatal to be in a place like that. Primarily a 'nonce' as they are hated by all and get hit whenever possible. Also their food got contaminated on a regular basis by bodily fluids and occasionally broken glass. The second thing was a grass as people with that title were treated as Jews with their yellow stars in Nazi Germany.

I wondered about standards in a place like that as every morning except Sunday we have our cells inspected with it being more in depth on Saturday. A failure resulted in a re-scrub. We had shaving mirrors of polished metal and once I was picked up for mine being dirty. What got me was that it was no dirtier than it had been the day before yet that day it passed and then the next day it failed. One way they tried to teach people about responsibility was on certain occasions if one person committed an offence the entire wing or, on the latest occasion, one side of it was punished. That time it was due to having being banged up for a significant length of time and so some people had thrown 'shit parcels' out the window to land in the courtyard. Some of those hardened criminals were surprisingly soft when it came to things like personal hygiene. They couldn't bear to be in their cell with their own stools for any length of time and so wrapped it in paper, tied it up with blanket string and launched it out the window. Because of one person doing that all of one side of the wing was deprived of their association for a night.

We had a potentially nasty situation when England and Wales had a game of rugby and it resulted in 25-6 to England. I think about a third of inmates there were from Wales and being beaten at rugby didn't do their morale any favours. In fact one got so unhappy about it he smashed up his cell and barricaded himself in. The screws chose to use brain rather than brawn to pacify the situation and extract the inmate which was probably a good idea as he had cut himself up a bit with either his razor blade or glass from the window.

One good way for a creative person like me to pass time was to try and express my feelings and emotions in poetry. If I was not feeling too original I found I could take a known piece of work and write a version with the same structure but new words. As we were at war with Iraq and Saddam Hussein at that time I took Lewis Carroll's '*The Hunting of the Snark*' and wrote a revised version called '*The Hunting of the Scud*' as those missiles were being constantly talked about on the radio. When I next saw the psychiatrist he just wanted to read my life story but I think it might have helped him understand me and my thinking if he read my poetry. Of course to do that he'd have to know I'd written it and he wouldn't do that unless he had a meaningful conversation with me which he hadn't managed by then. He said he was going to get the 'area forensic psychiatrist' to come and see me. He sounded clever and important and was probably even more distant and unapproachable than any psychiatrist I'd met yet. After all if the one at Moorhaven had got to know me better and given an accurate report at the trial I'd probably have been in a psychiatric unit in a specialised prison somewhere instead of the YOI for all criminals between 16 and 21.

Having done my time at boarding school I found the emotional aspect not too bad, but the physical features of my sentence were the most trying. We had a morning parade when all inmates grouped up on the yard and answered a roll call. I remember doing that in midwinter after having a shower and it being so cold that my hair froze full of icicles. The other real cold problem was when we had a clear night. I remember sitting up on my wardrobe on cloudless nights and watching showers of shooting stars over Portland Harbour. Then in the following morning there was a layer of ice on the inside of the window. These days I'm led to believe apparently a lot if not all prison cells have curtains and their own supplied TVs. One of the inmates' tricks in Portland was taking advantage of the heating pipes which ran through each cell via the walls separating the cells. People could write notes and then slip them through the gap where the pipe passed from one cell to the next. This was used to arrange deals for association time, for example what became called a HOD. This was a Half Ounce Deal swapping an individual half ounce packet of baccy for a couple of spliffs worth of cannabis. I must confess to taking advantage of such but nothing worse. I knew that was hardly ever in short supply but I don't know how much stronger stuff was available as it was out of my league in those days. I did know that in Exeter there was 'pink champagne' which is a kind of amphetamine, talk of LSD blotters coming in under postage stamps and I didn't know about heroin or coke back then.

One thing regarding intoxication which impressed me was when one of the kitchen workers was taken down to 'the block' for two weeks and was told he would have to do an extra couple of months out of his remission. He had used apples, sugar and yeast to make 'moonshine' in a bucket.

I used some of the abundant time on my hands to get rather better read. It seemed a good idea to read about other people's horrid prison situations to make mine seem more manageable. Therefore two books I had sent in to me were *One Day in the Life of Ivan Denisovich* and *Darkness at Noon*. These showed me how grateful I should be for having access to a smoke whenever I felt the need as I was much more fortunate than Shukov in Solzhenitsyn's story.

"Shukov had finished his last pinch of tobacco and saw no prospects of acquiring any more before evening. Every nerve in his body was taut, all his longing was concentrated in that fag-end – which meant more to him now, it seemed than freedom itself:"

I may have misheard or misunderstood but I got the impression that convicts can receive treatment which Prisoners of War weren't allowed to get due to the Geneva Convention. If the officers wanted to get information out of us we could be taken down to the punishment block but that shouldn't be done at Colditz or Tenko in theory. I tried to read *The Gulag Archipelago* while inside but found it too difficult especially when compared to *A Day in the Life of Ivan Denisovich*. I heard on the radio a quotation which makes me wonder about the French Navy and what happens when they work with us on NATO exercises as I could imagine our boys using this piece of humour to try and get a response. Apparently the motto of the French Navy is "A l'eau, c'est l'heure!" Meaning 'to the water, it is time' and sounding very like "'allo sailor!"

Latin wasn't my strong point at school but I could do enough to work out what is seen to be a real prison motto for both the inmates and those who work there. "Illegitemus non Carborundum", 'Don't let the bastards grind you down.' It turned out to be very appropriate as I discovered the phrase on the same day I had half an ounce of tobacco 'taxed' from my cell. Thinking of mottos and similar reminds me of something I found very trying about the writing of James

Joyce. *The Dubliners* is OK on this subject but *Ulysses* was the tiresome one as in it Mr Joyce regularly put in quotes in Latin and French without a translated version.

One thing which is a fundamental aspect of prison life is routine. Once you got indoctrinated with it you could usually get through each day without too much thinking. In some ways it's a good thing as thinking isn't a productive way to pass your time in there but it may become painfully repetitive. For example once you were familiar with it all you could tell what day of the week it was by what meal you got. Roast for Sunday's lunch and a salad in the evening, fish fingers or fillets in a good week on Friday evening having had stew for lunch. Someone made me laugh with a good little kind of pun relating to the meals. They described one of our stews and said it was made with 'chewing steak'. Like just about every main meal there it was served with cabbage that had been so seriously boiled it was almost pourable and couldn't be served using a draining spoon. If not with 'aqua-cabbage' then the meal would either have carrot in or with it. I knew some people who have been there for a significant length of time and so established some trust and so got to go and work on a local farm which I guessed was mass producing certain vegetables. Just occasionally we got an incredible meal which contains no cabbage or carrot and so it was surprising how happy some mashed swede could make you. It's surprising some of the routines we had which I couldn't see any reason for. Another strange one was if we wanted some toilet paper we had to get it from the association room and parade out with it. They may have believed in humanity in that place but not dignity, for sure.

I spent most of one day in my cell waiting to see the visiting area forensic psychiatrist. When I did eventually meet him I was not very impressed. For a start he really looked like a psychiatrist but what really disappointed me was I thought he might be clever and so ask me subtle questions rather than ones as delicate and refined as a baseball bat which I had heard a story about a few nights before from a young Welshman doing two and a half or so for the damage he had caused to his fiancée with it. The questions he asked were things such as, 'Do you think everyone is plotting against you?' and 'Do you think people are talking about you?' I don't know why he didn't just ask me if I suffered from paranoia as that was obviously what he wanted to know. I was very tempted to save him from asking me if I had a split personality by simply saying to him that I didn't think I was Napoleon, Caesar, Jesus or the King of England. It was all worthwhile as I confess I intentionally took our conversation very slowly and so managed to avoid PE which would have been very bad that day as it was snowing. The good thing about that though was that it didn't come in my window to the extent the rain did.

One thing which was particularly annoying there was that you are expected to know what standards are demanded without anyone ever telling you what they were. For example one day on a Governor's Inspection the officer decided to have a really close look at the cleaning kit I had which resulted in the following conversation.

"Bridgwater, why have you got four cloths here in your bucket?"

"What's that Sir? Oh, I've always had them as they were here when I was given the cell, Boss."

"That maybe so but why have you got a tin of metal polish? You had better not have been sniffing it!"

He put the tin in his pocket and gave me a very condemning look. There was something about the gaze that made me think he may well have previously been an Armed Forces NCO and it was supported by a very spartan Sergeant-Major style moustache.

"Why have you got two ashtrays boy? You aren't trying to be someone on this wing are you?"

"No Sir, I'm not looking to be a 'Daddy', in fact I don't even want to be a distant cousin."

"Well you're on 'minor report' and I'm going to tell the Senior Officer to keep an eye on you."

So I'd got four rags and two moulded pieces of plastic that you wouldn't pay for in a shop as the cheapest ashtrays anywhere would be considerably better than those. That seemed to make me a potential number one criminal on the wing.

The routine there was such a solid structure that it was quite a shocking surprise when something unexpected happens. Usually it turned out to be something unpleasant like being locked up when it should be association and it was due to people throwing parcels out the window or for a while it was due to officers being on strike. When one got a nice surprise it was such a bolt from the blue it could make you happy for a day or two after and one time I had something which put me in a good mood for the whole of the rest of the week. I was permitted one visit every four weeks and that was the rule so anything that overcame that was remarkable if it was successfully managed. My friend from home Rev. John had been in touch with the prison chaplain and so got permission to visit me privately one to one, separately from a visit requiring a Visiting Order. John was the kind of person everyone found easy to talk to and enjoy the company of so that time I had my most enjoyable three quarters of an hour since entering the establishment. He also managed to bring in some chocolate biscuits and gave me a book of Simon Drew pictures. Back then Mr Drew was an artist only known locally in Devon but since he has become known all over the country. He takes known phrases and changes them a little, and then does a cartoon style picture to go with the revised expression. For example 'God moves in mysterious ways' and 'Dark satanic mills' become 'Cod moves in mysterious ways' and 'Dark satanic moles' and illustrations showed peculiar fishy movements and moles digging out a place for devil worship.

Chapter 16

Another enjoyable surprise came the day after that, making that one of the best weeks I'd had for ages and I'd been behind bars seven months by then. I came back to my cell at lunch time and found I had a parcel from Miss B. Buckley which was a shock as to start with I couldn't remember who that was. Luckily the letter was signed Beth and that brought it back to me. She was a friendly lady at the church Dad and I went to round the corner from Dad's house. Either she cared for me more than I realised or maybe she was trying to make my dad cheer up. I knew that as she must have talked to him about where I was and how he and I were coping. The kind yet surprising thing she had done was she sent a Bridge book and yet she hadn't known I was a Bridge player. It was a good book as it had a story to it, it wasn't just a collection of deals in which to choose the best bidding and then focus on the card play. To make it more worthwhile what the author had done was create some interesting characters based on different animals and compose bizarre hands for them to play. She had also sent a few magazines of logic problems which were something I'd not come across before. They were more interesting than I predicted and may well have helped my thinking patterns, especially with regard to the GCSE statistics I was preparing for to fill my maths classes.

As part of our weekday routine we had a long, slow parade which was seriously painful by the end if it was a winter one. It was very cold and uncomfortable but what made it so bad was that being up on the extremity of Portland Bill we really caught the roaring gales as they came up the channel. I didn't think that was by chance, but definitely designed as HMP Dartmoor was intentionally in the most inhospitable area of Devon. If I was going to be there for the rest of my sentence, which I expected, I hoped I could establish some trust and get made an orderly. The orderlies had a bit more freedom and were allowed to walk from one wing to another without being escorted. However the real things that made a difference were that they got a donkey jacket which was a lot more insulated than the denim jackets most of us wore. Also they got to make drinks for the screws and so they got their own chance to make a brew and so could have a cup of tea which hadn't gone cold and brewed longer than a session of 'bang up.' These days every cell has facilities for beverages and that's one reason I think prison is a joke these days. I really wondered about the desperation of some people there as they must have had some frighteningly strong motivation to do certain things. It may be the same on the inside or the outside. For example some people tried to escape to avoid a confrontation with a particular inmate and some tried it because they had hidden a quantity of money and feared another gang member would get hold of it, perhaps because the associate has already been released and was not trusted. That came to mind as we had no TV on one evening as the guards were patrolling the Isle of Portland looking for an escapee, and he must have been frantic to try and abscond in that day's weather. Biting cold wind with showers of snow and so much cloud cover it had been fairly dark grey for days which matched with the granite the place was built of.

The more time I was in there, the more respect I had for the Russians, particularly those who Stalin had committed to the gulag as it's phenomenal how much cold they had to tolerate. We often had mornings which greeted us with ice on the inside of the windows and no real cleaning or 'slopping out' as the water pipes in the recesses had frozen solid. Being in my cell wearing all the clothes I had I still felt cold and then when we got association a stupid unexplained rule came into action. When on association we were allowed to wear our jackets but not our sweatshirts. I couldn't find out why and it just seemed totally pointless. That's a typical example of the prison system which I was beginning to take on board and get familiar with by then. Just to rub it in, though I'm sure it wasn't on purpose to make me jealous, I received a postcard from my mum's side of the family, the Robinsons, one day saying that they were currently on a cruise ship in the Caribbean for their first holiday of that year. Still like most things in life the 'big freeze' did have its sort of silver lining and in that case it was that it shut up the seagulls. They were so unpopular there that in the spring there was a working party put up on the roof to smash up the eggs and so reduce the population. I know some of us wondered if it would be worth collecting and then eating the eggs, but we were worried they'd taste fishy. Maybe not a good flavour but probably a better texture than powdered egg. It was so cold in the mornings that when we had cornflakes rather than porridge we used to get ice crystals in our milk which gave a crunch to the soggy cereal.

I did wonder then, and still do now, about justice and the sentencing which different crimes and offenders receive. One thing I was puzzled about then was that I got three years when I attacked and hurt somebody but not really with any vindictive motive and I wasn't out to hurt that person in particular. A guy that was moved into Nelson wing got eighteen months for killing someone by reckless driving and in that case it seemed to have been intentional not just by accident. A motorcar was a very good murder weapon as killing by reckless driving only got three years maximum I think whereas obviously life is the obligatory sentence for murder. Then of course there's the debate about should life mean till you pass away or just do a few years till the authorities think you aren't going to be a risk to the general public.

Obviously by definition the criminals in the establishment were those who were either unlucky or not very good, as otherwise they wouldn't have been caught. Apart from me as basically I felt guilty and so told the local coppers what I had done, but had gone in to a bit too much detail. I heard a good example of bad luck and how one can undergo a serious of events which will result in feeling gutted. A Bristol guy had been driving away from his third, and what was planned to be his last, armed robbery with all his loot and his gun in the car boot. He was pulled over for not having an up to date tax disc which was one of the first things he had really meant to purchase with his ill-gotten gains. He was taken to the police station to make a statement yet he managed to play things cool regardless of all the evidence still in his car. He thought he was going to pull it all off as he walked out of the police station reception just as the woman worker from the Post Office he had robbed came in to give a statement and recognised him and so immediately called the nearest officer to arrest him. Therefore he got a few years rather than just a tax disc fine.

The establishment was very much ruled by the survival of the fittest laws which had been promoted by Mr Darwin. The thing that made it particularly hard to deal with was that people changed from placid, tranquil individuals who could be taken to a vicar's tea party to violent, malicious, hate-the-whole-world beings that made the eponymous star of 'Alien' seem like good company. I was in one of the main classrooms one day watching two guys having what started off as a slightly heated discussion and within seconds it had escalated to a battle for existence. I wouldn't have minded too much if they kept it to themselves but soon there were chairs flying through the air which resulted in me getting bruised and my calculator being broken beyond repair. Also that day I had been expecting to talk to somebody from one of the other wings. If I remember correctly he was called Greg and lived in Drake house. All seven wings there were named after significant naval officers so we also had Grenville, Benbow, Rodney and Raleigh as well as Nelson where I was and Hardy which everyone spent a couple of weeks in for introduction. However he didn't turn up and then when I did see him after the weekend he had one of the worst black eyes I'd ever seen. People don't do their thuggery by half measures in a place like that. When I did get to talk to Greg he wasn't feeling very talkative. I could certainly agree with a phrase he was saying describing how he had been feeling. "There is no greater sorrow than recalling a time of happiness when in misery."

It seemed to me that prison officers generally could get messages which were given to them subtly but they usually took a long time to actually take them on board. I made hints and comments about the condition my cell was in and that I'd like to go to one which wasn't so susceptible to the elements. At inspection one morning the officer unlocked the door but instead of then checking for dust and seeing how neatly I've folded my clothes and bed pack he just looked round and then said, "This cell really should be condemned." However I was never moved out of it until I was released. Maybe if I had complained about it I would have gone to another but it was hard to tell what was worth complaining about and what was prison standard and so if you made an issue of it you were just being a 'wet muppet'.

At one time I was so fed up with it all I gave suicide a serious period of thought for a few days. There's about one try every week or so and one successful attempt a month. I could certainly have imagined that life would seem an even more appalling option if I didn't have some friends and family who I knew cared about me and my future waiting for me on the outside. I got the impression from chats I had with a number of different people in different situations that a large number of guys in there had grown up in care homes or with particularly dysfunctional families. It certainly seemed to fit in with all the sociology statistics I had previously been told on *Panorama* and similar.

It was incredible what provided inspiration for poetry writing as on a cold, wet, dark evening I was motivated to do a first draft of a piece which I was driven to write by hearing a foghorn. Still it certainly worked just taking what ever came to mind rather than picking a subject and trying to write about it on demand. All my best pieces were written when something came to my head and so I wrote about it rather than I thought of a particular topic and tried to write an item relating to it. The first poem I remember winning a prize with was done for Mr Hunter at Plymouth College. I was a day boy at the time and so saw a lot of my cat Brum who had a slightly deformed nose and so was always sniffing and sneezing. I wrote a poem in which she sneezed on my supper and it won me a Mars bar. I thought Mars bars were disgustingly sickly sweet and I hated them so I never bought one myself but it was the fact I'd won it with a piece of my poetry that made it significant. I discovered I'd be able to enter a few of my poems in the Koestler Awards as the trust set up by Arthur Koestler was a charity which supports prison inmates and detained psychiatric patients in the UK giving them the opportunity to express themselves creatively. It was ironic as when I did an access course about ten years later for my project I compared Koestler's book *Darkness at Noon* with Solzhenitsyn's *One day in the life of Ivan Denisovich* and Koestler was a Hungarian which was the country I went to and did my teaching in.

One day we had a better than usual lesson as our maths teacher was occupied and also most of the students were busy doing their RSA Literacy tests. The result was just a couple of us in a class in which a different from usual teacher talked about psychology/philosophy and how it relates to happiness and personality. It was hard to be sure but I got the impression that some of the teachers there thought we spent a lot of time considering philosophical issues while alone in our cells. I think such things were probably above most inmates there but I did consider things like God and other big questions. The teacher talked about Karl Popper and Abraham Maslow which I found fascinating but I doubt the others got so much from it.

"No man is an island, entire of itself." John Donne wrote that in 1624 and despite being the kind of person who would be described as quite a loner I was inclined to agree with him. Being an only child with only one parent since I was five years old I had become very familiar and content with my own company and I must confess that for longer than average I had an imaginary friend. Just to make things more interesting my invisible companion hadn't been a boy like me but was a playful black dragon called 'Jet'. Portland is called an island but is permanently attached to the mainland by an isthmus. It is so narrow that a couple of screws could easily guard it and make sure no escaped prisoner passed along it on their way to freedom. All in all I thought slightly more than half the time I was there I was glad there were other people there to share the suffering with. The idea of doing a sentence alone like Rudolph Hess did appeal sometimes though. Occasionally someone I knew from Exeter arrived and usually they were not very high on my list of worthwhile companions. In fact, one turned up one day that I'd put at the top of the list of individuals I wished were paralysed from the eyebrows down. Even if no man is an island I think I was probably the human equivalent to Portland, having very limited links with society yet, despite usually being able to get through a day without a word to or from anyone, I needed to talk to someone to do what I did on a few occasions. For example when I had the confidence and enough tobacco in hand to go and organise an HOD. Now it may have been similar to a prison urban myth, but what people said was that a lot of the screws didn't mind inmates smoking 'hash' as it encouraged them to be more passive and chilled out. Especially as some of those who were in the Pucklechurch riots of Bristol have been sent here to Portland. I was told some screws had come into cells, particularly ones which had more than one resident and if there was a suspicious smell or the roll up in someone's hand looked shockingly large they've said open the window and they would be back in five minutes. To utilise my helping of cannabis to best effect I listened to *Equinox* by Jean-Michel Jarre having smoked it, so with eyes closed I could imagine being anywhere - from a live Paris concert to the psychedelic type of planet Captain Kirk and crew used to visit.

Chapter 17

Despite being a regular church goer while living with my dad before my unorthodox gap year started, and being a well-established member of the Stoke Damerel congregation these days, I chose not to go to chapel while I was in Portland. I suppose that was a bit hypocritical in some ways as I used to get my vicar from home to come and give me extra visits as I've already mentioned. The reason I didn't like chapel at Portland was due to one of the three different types of chapel goers there were there in my opinion. First were those who did it because they believed and so were sincere. I found out in a debate we had one afternoon in the education department that either it was a surprisingly high number of believers or there were a lot of people lying about their extent of belief. Secondly, a number did it just to escape an hour or two of bang-up on Sundays which could often be the most boring day of a very boring week. I felt sympathy for both of these groups but the ones I really didn't like, and in fact was disgusted by, were those who used it as a significant chance to chat with people from a different wing to themselves. In a way these guys annoyed me as much as what my school chaplain called 'four wheeled Christians.' These are the people who first turn up with a pram to baptise their infant as it's the family tradition not because they see it as an essential activity to result in lifelong forgiveness and eternal life. If this kind of service is being performed at my local church I don't turn up as I believe people should choose to be baptised themselves and the best baptism I've ever been to was a total emersion ceremony for a born again Christian friend of mine who was a teenager at the time. I've also thought about arranging a baptism for myself by my choice, as I have been confirmed but there is nothing in the Bible giving that any meaning. After a gap of about twenty-five years the "four wheeled Christians" turned up again making an appearance in a Rolls Royce or a horse drawn carriage for their marriage. Then eventually a final show up in a Hearse for their funeral.

I and a few others got selected to form a group who would meet a psychologist once a week and we could try and discuss any emotional issues we had which we thought may have been contributory factors to getting us locked up. I didn't know about the history of the others but I reckon I was selected as, from a psychiatric viewpoint, watching your mum go through a windscreen and die when you're aged five when there's nobody else there is going to be traumatic. The especially disturbing element of it in my opinion was that as there were no other cars on the scene and nothing seemed to have failed on the car we were in, so I assumed for years I had done something distracting and so I was responsible for the fatal crash. Following that I feel I must have had a childhood which had a very limited number of hugs and cuddles. It didn't bother me back then but now I sometimes feel I'm almost physically aching for a hug or a cuddle and at times I can't help wondering when I last had one and who it was from. It may have been Dad but being a naval officer from a family with a history of boarding schools and military correctness, I know he has never really seen physical contact as something excessively required.

Some of the guys in that 'psycho' group had quite isolated upbringings for various reasons. One boy was only sixteen yet he was locked in there already, having been involved in crime at the children's home he had been living in. He and quite a few others had been in care since as far back as they could remember. Another lad was twenty-two years old and was behind bars for the eighth time. We had an interesting almost entertaining conversation when we went out for a fag break half way through one psycho session. I was reminded of the Monty Python sketch with the Yorkshire men talking about their childhoods and the conditions they had to endure, each one getting worse and more extreme. The boys who had been in care did the same thing, but because nobody else could confirm or deny what they claimed, I thought some of them got a bit exaggerated.

I didn't expect anybody to start opening up and showing their feelings at the group, but I was very surprised when one who I thought would be particularly withdrawn began explaining how he had suffered at home due to alcoholic parents and then taking solvent himself. He didn't have to go very far before it was clear some of the others could relate to what he was saying and in minutes he was crying his eyes out and others were clearly on the edge of an emotional flood, trying to hold it all in. People really can't be judged by appearances, particularly there. There was a lad who looked very trim and proper, the kind of person I'd hang around with on the outside, yet he'd spent ages living on the street in a squat and shoplifting gas then alcohol on a daily basis. He had just been moved there from another YOI as his friend and cell mate in his previous place had committed suicide. He was the kind of person who reinforced the expression a Cornish friend of mine regularly uses- 'Don't judge an orange by its skin.' Curious that that came from Cornwall, as oranges aren't indigenous. In some ways I suppose I am a good example of the same as having gone to a Prep school then a private boarding establishment till I was eighteen I spoke very well without trying to and unlike most people locked up there I was happy on Sundays when we had to wear shirt and tie. I'm not the kind of person you'd expect to have a lifelong criminal record for a violence offence.

Thinking about it though, it's often the intellectuals who become the serial killers such as Drs Shipman and Lecter show.

I don't know if it was thanks to the psychologist running the group, or just that after a while I was more familiar with the other members of the group, but we had a session talking about past events which we felt had a major effect on who we were. I was surprised to find that by the end I had given a detailed description of the car accident and had had a lengthy weeping session myself. I only know about it now because I wrote it in my prison diary. It really is a thing for the diary when I or my dad shed a tear. I could probably count on one hand the times each of us can recall seeing the other crying. After that in the 'psycho group' we were shown a relaxation technique but it didn't work very well due to our environment. Despite it being June at that moment it was still so cold that I was shivering while trying to relax both my body and mind. Also when in my cell I could see my breath condense in those days.

I decided that spending time in that establishment was such an unpleasant experience I wanted to get it all done in 'one sitting', so to speak. If I had a painful operation I needed to undergo at the dentist I'm the sort of person who would rather have one long very painful afternoon instead of two shorter less agonising afternoons. The reason I mention this is I decided I was not even going to apply for pre-parole leave. That was a short break over a long weekend in which a prisoner got to return home for a day or two unless there's a very good reason for them not to. Most people took it up but I thought it would be so depressing having to leave the place and then come back in again I decided not to go out but just get through it all in one go. Some people felt it was crazy but that's what I thought about anyone who left knowing they were going to be back in a few days later.

As I've mentioned, good visits and quality letters from friends and family are worth their weight in gold in there, but what I've never really thought about till now, years later is what everything was like for the people at the other end of the line. It can't have been a very enjoyable thing for them having breakfast when a letter of mine arrived telling them how I hated the cold, runny porridge I started the day with. Then, as they prepared to leave their warm central heated homes they would have just read about me in my cell which wasn't wind or waterproof. I've tried to remember what sort of mood my poems were in as I usually try not to write too depressingly. I wish I still had access to those poems as then I could see the ones I had entered in to the Koestler Trust awards and I could see which one I had read to my dad on one visit that had brought a tear to his eye. Back in those days my writing was just about one hundred percent poetry and letters, not short stories and potential plays and a novel as it has been since then. I wish I still had the poems of those days, as I know I wrote a good one using prison slang which I can't remember much of these days. One phrase which stuck in my memory was that everyone wanted 'jam.' This is a piece of rhyming slang being 'jam roll' rhyming with parole. Some words and phrases were ones I invented myself and used in my diary or when talking to myself which was a frequent pastime. I used to talk about 'flexi-toast' which we often had for breakfast. I described it as appearing as real toast yet bending and being rip-proof like a sheet of Gortex. The real curious property of it was that it behaved like laminated paper sheets and so was impossible to tear or rip and needed a serious concentration of effort and equipment to cut. As we only had plastic knives, teeth or razor blades were needed. One phrase which I held close to my heart for quite a while was one we invented ourselves in the classes. We described things as being 'flowered up' as we at the education department had creative sessions in which some people drew, some did technical drawing and some did woodwork. A couple of my classmates got very good at drawing intricate designs of ivy like plants with insects and other woodland creatures found entwined in them. These were either used for frames of pictures or to decorate woodwork products. Not being too ambitious in that field, I did little more than make a box on wheels and then a couple of kitchen utensils. I asked one of the more artistic guys to 'flower up' my box on wheels for me so it was decorated with unique quality patterns using a black marker pen before I applied varnish.

I'm very grateful to the young man from Tamworth who was in a cell just down the landing from where I was. He introduced me to some music which as I became more familiar with it developed to be just about my favourite complete album of music. It is *The Final Cut* by Pink Floyd. The band's bass player wrote pretty much all of it as can also be said of *The Wall*. He also wrote an opera about the French Revolution called '*Ca Ira*' which means 'There is hope.' Roger Waters was the best writer of both lyrics and music combined in the band, as he did those and later went on to do some quality solo albums such as '*The Pros and Cons of Hitch-hiking.*' I must confess to having a real weak spot for Mr Waters as not only has he written so much good stuff, I think he is one of the few artists who has managed to do a cover which is better than the original. What I'm thinking of is his version of '*Knockin' on Heaven's Door*' which is by Bob Dylan as everyone knows. When people wrote good lyrics, as I would say both of those guys did, I see it as poetry set to music rather than song lyrics. I know some people such as Jim Morrison and Nick Cave wrote both separately and there was a time when my musical friend Mike had seen some of my poetry and had plans to set it to music, but unfortunately that never happened. Quite how to define the difference between lyrics and poetry lines I've never mastered. Trent Reznor, the singer from Nine Inch Nails who is trained as a classical pianist often did poetry to music in my opinion.

I didn't know a thing about it till much later but after I got out and spent some time being a boyfriend and a 'culture vulture' I developed my interest in classical music. When I was growing up my great aunt used to regularly take me to see Glyndebourne touring opera and now and then I attended a concert by the Bournemouth Symphony orchestra. I'm very pleased with the way I learnt about classical music as it is as if I followed a 'Teach Yourself' course which I designed myself. I always enjoyed string quartets and orchestras from Radio 3 but till I studied it I didn't know what was what and who was who.

It all took off when someone like Simon Rattle was doing a music documentary which I happened to catch one day. I suddenly heard music which sounded very reminiscent of *'Jaws'* theme music yet the TV picture was a frozen Russian wasteland and I found out after a brief interlude that I'd just heard part of *The Rite of Spring* by Igor Stravinsky. It had been very enjoyable music so I got myself a copy of it from my local music and drama library where I had already become a regular taking out music like Queen, The Stranglers and copying them onto tapes as that was what I'd done while at school in the eighties. Since then I've pretty much taught myself about the great composers of classical music with a book in one hand and a CD case in the other. I must admit that over the last decade or so since one of my uncles knows I like that sort of thing he has introduced me to some class classical music by sending me CDs as Christmas presents. My favourite of those is probably Lutoslawski. I think my uncle particularly enjoys John Adams as he has sent me at least three albums of his music. He didn't send me the first piece of John Adams music I got to know however. That was *The Death of Klinghoffer*. If I remember rightly that got my attention when it was played once at Christmas, as the controllers like to give out a dose of cultural programs at that time of year. To start with I was used to operas all being very much about fictitious events in the past so I was curious about the subject of that one, and then when watching it on BBC2 I was impressed by the use of modern language. I was surprised to hear a baritone come out with the line *"You pour gasoline over women passengers on the bus to Tel Aviv and burn them alive, you don't give a shit."* Another great discovery regarding classical music occurred when I once took my dad out for his birthday to hear a string quartet and we bumped into someone he knew as usually happens when we go to any concert or performance these days. We got talking about lesser known high quality composers and via that route I was introduced to the fantastic Estonian composer Arvo Part, who is my choice living composer these days. I did enjoy the music I got to listen to while I was locked away but I'm glad words have always been my passion rather than numbers or music. While behind bars I was thinking of using my 'A' levels to go to university and study psychology. So I used that part of my life to do some serious people watching. As one of my friends in the education department was doing a correspondence course in psychology, I borrowed his text books when they were free. One of his books I spent some time browsing was *The Science of Mind and Behaviour*. I suppose I was being watched from a psychological point of view without realising it. I think that now because a couple of days before I was released I had a really good one to one talk with Mrs C., the head of the education department. During that she told me she had a degree in psychology as well as her teaching qualification but she didn't want to distract me from my science 'A' levels and that was why she hadn't told me about it previously.

I was very interested in the fact Howard Jacobson has won the Orange literature prize in 2010, as I read a book by him in 1991 called *Redback* which I found very amusing. I was also able to use my time back then to get more familiar with some classic novels such as a couple by Thomas Hardy. While there I read *Tess of the D'Urbervilles* and *The Mayor of Castorbridge* - very appropriate for while I was in that part of the country, as that area was what Hardy referred to as

Wessex. All the towns in his novels were based on real places as I know Castorbridge came from Dorchester.

Back then I did, and still do, find it disconcerting how quickly I can go from being full of the joys of life to feeling like I've been attacked by what Winston Churchill would call a 'black dog' episode. I had one day when I received some uplifting letters before going off to classes, and as it was sunny with an encouraging blue sky most people about were happy or at least not miserable as they sometimes got. However I went down to the lowest level of cheerfulness when I returned to my cell for lunch as I soon found out I had been completely taxed. My burn, phone card and personal stereo had all been lifted and so I'd have weeks without a radio which I found very distressing. However I was about as inspired as I could be by what happened the day after so then I was flying up in the clouds again. I had received my report from the education department which said I was "conscientious, quiet, pleasant, polite and unassuming." It also told me I wrote good poetry which was probably the best part of it all. To bring me back down after such an 'ego trip' I got a 'spin' the day after that. That was when everything in the cell was closely examined to see what I was hiding. They really did check everything in detail as all my books and letters were opened up and unfolded and then thrown out on to the landing as were all the other things I had. Also my sheets, blankets, clothes were investigated intimately particularly along the seams. Pictures got taken off the walls, the tubular metal constructing a chair and the bed got checked, the window bars solidity was confirmed and just to conclude the fun I received a very intimate strip search examining my hair, my nose, ears and everywhere else you can imagine. However I did feel like I had succeeded as the one thing I shouldn't have had was a razor blade and I kept that in a wafer thin crack in the wall which hadn't been noticed.

Sunday mornings were usually good for a couple of reasons. Firstly because there was no inspection, and also because we didn't start till an hour later than every other day. As I've said, despite being a significant thing before and after 'doing my bird' I didn't go to church then. One day was a particularly heavy duty memory session as I heard the congregation singing 'Magnificat' and it reminded me of being an altar boy/server in the ancient Saxon church at Bradford on Avon and also with my family friend Rev. John in the sixties architecture church at home. One thing he had done in Communion which I had really liked was using a real bread roll rather than the cardboard wafers usually used.

Chapter 18

I had been getting worried that when we were on summer holiday from the education department I would have weeks with nothing but 'bang-up' and also less wages. I got £2:90 or so when doing classes which was just adequate but that would go to £2:20 or so if I was in my cell all day. Then I wouldn't be able to buy enough burn, papers, matches and a packet of biscuits or a dark chocolate Bounty as I desired at canteen. Late one Monday morning in July I thought I had a far-reaching stint of time behind a closed door and it would be especially unpleasant till I had arranged a new radio, ideally with a Walkman tape player too. The weeks ahead of me made me feel like a nomad leaving an oasis knowing he has a very long, drawn out trying journey ahead which is unavoidable and can't be made easier by a significant amount. Then the senior wing officer opened my cell door.

"Would you like to get some fresh air, Bridgwater?" he inquired.

Being keen not to spend too much time in a room where I could almost touch the side walls by standing in the centre with my arms stretched out and about two and a half stretches from end to end I confirmed immediately. It turned out to be a very productive decision. I was given a place on the garden work detail. To start with I had a job weeding the prison gardens which meant I had plenty of time to enjoy being out in the open, and as it started in July and continued throughout August by the time it was all over I had acquired a good suntan, which is not something I expected to receive while being detained at Her Majesty's pleasure. I think doing the basic gardening routine was a bit of a test as to whether or not I could be trusted without a pair of eyes on me constantly, as not long after I was taken outside the main walls to the playing fields where I was given the task of Groundsman on the cricket pitch. Mostly that involved cutting the grass, paying special attention to the 'square' in the centre. I also had to go round the edge drawing the oval shaped white line and mark out the creases. Despite it being about as enjoyable a job as I could have hoped for, there was however one task involved in it all which was very physically draining and lead to me getting terrible blisters on my hands despite wearing thick gloves. The pitch was located on a flat area surrounded by a steep downward slope so it was like it was the stage of an amphitheatre. To cut the grass on the slope I had to get a Flymo and tie it on the end of a rope. Then I had stand at the top of the slope and lower the grass cutter down, pull it up again and carry on in the same way all around the 'dell' as I called it. Clearly I was very trusted by the screws by then as I was outside the prison wall most of the day and out of reach of everyone unless they made a determined effort to track me down. I may be wrong but I think once I'd made it clear I could handle being inside and I agreed with Evelyn Waugh's philosophy regarding it and time in public school, the officers understood I would just get my head down and do it. Being outside the main wall I can't deny I thought about absconding but it didn't seem a good idea to me. For a few days I seriously wondered what would happen if I was out working and I got 'kidnapped'. Would that count as an abscond or would they just pick things up from my length of time already served when I came back into custody. This played on my mind as I had a couple of friends who I felt I could persuade to 'kidnap' me on request so I could arrange when and where for them to capture me and then 'hold' me for a long weekend, after which I'd 'escape' and hand myself back into custody. However that would be no different from the pre-parole leave scheme which didn't appeal to me.

Portland certainly is quite a place as far as weather conditions go, as I can recall days which would have been in August when it was so foggy in the afternoon I could be at one end of the cricket square and I couldn't see the other end, so I had a very difficult job ensuring that I kept travelling in a straight line parallel with the other ones so I could get the stripes going up and down like one sees on a well-manicured lawn. On days like that I often used to meet up with the inmates from The Verne, which was adult low security prison on the island, as they had access to a shed like structure which allowed us to get out of the moisture laden atmosphere and get indoors to have a cup of tea and a burn.

Reminiscence and nostalgia are very curious things which I think I may understand better when I'm an old man. One day I was out cutting the grass around the cricket pitch when I noticed an OAP looking person walking about and watching me and my actions in a rather inquiring manner. Eventually he came over to me as I think he realised he was making me feel uncomfortable and he started talking.

"You're one of the lads from the YOI aren't you?" he started.

"Yes. That's right," I replied.

"You've got my sympathy mate," he said smiling and gazing vacantly into the middle distance. He then explained that in 1953 he had come to Benbow House to do a two year ten month stretch. This was the first time he had been back to Portland since then as he was having a holiday travelling to places which had been significant during his younger years and showing them to his wife. We talked for a while and he said it had been a Borstal back then and I've got the impression from that conversation and some I've had with a friend of mine who is ten years older than me and also has experience of time behind bars that it was really quite violent and brutal back then. I didn't feel it was a holiday camp in my days, but we were having a walk in the park compared to the previous generations. People still got hung back then, and homosexuality was a crime everywhere not just on the Isle of Man as it is these days.

Some Thursday mornings I didn't get let out to go to work and I knew those were the days I was going to have a chat with the visiting psychiatrist. Despite having a double barrelled name and dressing like Sir Robin Day, I usually found him quite a reasonable bloke. However one time he did piss me off as he had a student with him who I had agreed could join us as I didn't see how it could be a problem. However I got the feeling the doctor was 'displaying' me like an unfortunate disease victim such as The Elephant Man or some such 'freak' in the days of the Victorian peepshows.

Reputations count for a lot in those sorts of places. They usually took a long time to build up and relied on having a good history of being violent, not grassing on anyone and being a pain in the arse to all authority encountered since early childhood. Obviously what you were in for and what you had either been convicted for previously or had got away with in the past was significant too. One guy I knew was very highly regarded for having had fights with screws and other inmates and having been to numerous institutions before the one we were in then. He wasn't a 'Daddy' to use the title from the film 'Scum' which starred Ray Winstone and which I only saw after my time inside, but he was not to be crossed or questioned by people who knew any of the basic principles of self-preservation. However, I never saw somebody of high esteem drop as fast as he did once a particular fact came to light. I don't understand how it appeared from nowhere but one day a newspaper cutting suddenly turned up revealing he was not inside for armed robbery as he had led us all to believe, yet he was accused of being a 'nonce' - either a rapist or he had sexually assaulted a child or a vulnerable adult. The news spread across the whole place from wall to wall with terrifying speed and he was immediately moved to the punishment block so he could be watched over 24/7 for his own protection. Next day he was transferred out and he may well have gone to somewhere that had a wing devoted to people imprisoned under the dreaded Rule 43 which was for grasses, nonces and anyone else who might be at risk out in the general prison population.

Usually the films and videos we saw in the education department didn't do much to or for me and, as often as not, they were things I already knew about or I had seen the film before anyway. However one film we saw had a lasting effect on my conscience and I still reflect on it these days more than twenty years later. It was called "Fourteen Days in May" and was the true life documentary about an American called Edward Earl Johnson who was a Mississippian black man convicted of murder. He spent seven years on 'death row' protesting his innocence to the last day. The film was about his last fourteen days of life, his execution, and how some evidence was found just two days later which certified his innocence. It was reminiscent of '*To Kill a Mocking Bird*' which I had studied at GCSE English literature and which also made a good film starring Gregory Peck. He also gave a first class performance in *Moby Dick* which is another good film based on a high quality piece of literature in my opinion. Sometime later we saw a film called '*The Journey*' which was a follow up to the previous film which confirmed the man's innocence and showed how all those who had investigated at the time did all they could to ignore the accumulation of salvaging evidence. Another trip down memory lane I had with the help of a piece of literature was when we had a play reading session in an English class and out came '*The Long, The Short and the Tall*' which I had also done at GCSE. I did wonder who chose which videos to show us as one day we got to see a documentary about shotguns and then a second one about Lee Enfield .303 rifles which I already knew a bit about having used one in the CCF at school. Considering there are a load of laws saying that people with criminal records are not allowed to have anything to do with firearms, it seems a curious thing to show us films about.

I probably read more while in Portland than I have ever done in the same length of time before or since. A lot of it was limited to what the prison library contained but I did have a few books sent to me, either ones I requested or things people thought I would like. It was a very good environment for poetry reading, as poems are best read out loud, which I could do at my leisure while in my cell. One particularly good source of such was *The Oxford Book of Contemporary Verse. 1945-1980.* I was particularly impressed by certain poem titles I came across in that book such as *Excerpt from a Report to the Galactic Council, Autobiography of a Lungworm* and *Examination at the Womb-door.* It was also while there I discovered someone who has grown to be a favourite writer of mine in his genre of Gothic fiction. That's H.P. Lovecraft, who Stephen King calls 'the 20th century horror story's dark and baroque Prince.'

I didn't usually pay much attention to the art classes, but used them as a chance to sit at the back and study cytology or whatever topic seemed to need working on for my 'A' level biology. However once we had a lesson when we were shown a video about how to paint with water colours. Certainly it was not my subject, but the artist was out on Dartmoor painting Hay Tor which is a place I was very familiar with. I had walked round it when out doing Dartmoor Letterboxing, and we had climbed it in the army cadets when out with a retired Royal Marine doing our outdoor activities. That also brought back some unpleasant memories as with him we had also done canoeing. As a basic concept that was fine, but it took on a different level on the pain-pleasure scale when we went down the River Dart one January looking at the icicles on the river bank. If some memories get 'burnt in' those were 'frozen in'.

An interesting quote I heard on the radio around that time was 'a neurotic is someone who builds castles in the sky, a psychotic lives in them and a psychiatrist collects the rent.' One thing I certainly learnt while there was how little you can tell about someone's internal mental condition by outward appearances. A Welshman a few cells along the landing from me seemed to be having a ball as he worked in the kitchen and so had plenty of food and having been inside previously he was known by the screws and they would get him to make and deliver their tea which meant he had pretty much free access to hot drinks and biscuits. He was never short of any supplies and had numerous Welsh friends in all the wings and in other prisons. However one day he decided to cut his wrists and got in quite a condition as his cell bell didn't work which he hadn't known due to having the door open most of the time.

I really do have questions regarding the sentences people get given by the judges of this country, as back in those days on the radio I heard of two sixteen year old boys who got twelve months each for manslaughter having beaten another boy to death. I had a neighbour who got four years for conspiracy to robbery yet he never actually physically committed a crime.

I had a unique experience completely out of the blue one day when a screw came over to me when I was at the hospital wing picking up my morning medication. He said he was going to take me into Weymouth to see the local neurologist about my epilepsy. So I got handcuffed to the screw and taken down in a taxi, then had to walk through the hospital feeling like a dog on a lead as the officer walked along with his arm trailing behind him as though he was dragging along a load of contaminated rubbish. I confess that was one of the few times I really resented the way I was treated by a prison officer. We got to the waiting room and were sat as far from the door as possible. It was quite obvious that our presence was making all the other patients more than a little uncomfortable. There were young children cowering behind their parents and clearly I was being compared to a 'bogeyman' as mums were saying to their little boys and girls that if they didn't behave and take their medicine they would end up like me.

There was a pre-release course for about a week which all inmates were meant to go on, but for some reason I never did it. I expect it was because probation and others knew I had a welcoming family to go back to and that I wouldn't be going out with the idea of getting a heroin hit being principal in my mind. As my release day approached I got more and more restless, short tempered and found it just about impossible to sleep. I was however very capable of lying on my bed and daydreaming about what things would be like when I was back in the real world.

When actual release day was reached I had not had any sleep for the last few days and when I went down to reception at 6:30 on Thursday 5th December 1991 I don't think I had ever felt so highly strung. Certainly not on the day I was sentenced, as that had been on the horizon for ages and had approached with unavoidable inevitability. Release; I couldn't believe until it actually happened and I was outside the walls of Portland YOI, not being instructed or watched over by a prison officer. As they didn't like to just throw you out of the door and leave rubbish on their forecourt they took me and a couple of others also out on the same day down to Portland town square where we were left with our release grant, any money we had on us when we were first taken in and a travel permit if we had asked for one.

I looked around in a state of shock, feeling very disconnected to everything. I didn't have the routine and structure of prison life to 'support' me anymore and I didn't feel at all integrated into modern society and culture. Then I saw my dad's car pull up at the bus stop about fifty meters in front of me. Regardless of being properly brought up and having previously always tried very hard indeed to avoid swearing in front of my father I ran towards him at full velocity shouting at maximum volume, "I'm fucking free! I've fucking done it!"

Partly because I thought they would make interesting mementos to show people in later days and also because I knew it would annoy the people working there, the first thing I did was get Dad to drive me back up to the main gate with the camera I'd asked him to bring on the morning I was released. I took some pictures of the main gate and the gargantuan wall surrounding the whole establishment and within minutes a screw came over and as politely as he could he told me to 'Fuck off!' They said they thought I wanted the photos to help me plan an escape but I think I did it just so I could look at them later to convince myself it had really happened, as it still seemed very unbelievable in some ways.

Dad and I were glad to leave the Isle of Portland and go to a greasy spoon cafe for what I saw as the first quality breakfast for over five hundred days. Just the novelty of being able to make my own choices of what to eat and how to have it cooked was almost overwhelming. Next on our itinerary for that day was the little village of Holt which was where we lived when Mum had the car accident. She was buried in the tiny church's graveyard and we paid our respects then looked at the cottage which had been our home and finished the visit with lunch at the local pub.

Chapter 19

Thinking of scars always reminds me of two things. The primary one being the most memorable and recognisable scar I remember having ever seen. When I was on remand at HMP Exeter in the young offenders' wing I met a Glaswegian who really sounded like Rab C. Nesbit, not that he had been heard of then. The Scotsman in Exeter had had one of his ears cut off by an old fashion style razor blade. He didn't have a hole in the side of his head but instead had a line of scar tissue from just behind his temple to halfway down his neck. It generally didn't seem to bother him, but what did piss him off was when other inmates, particularly the Scousers, mocked his use of headphones when listening to a personal stereo, yet obviously he only heard things in mono. The other thing that comes to mind regarding scars is self-inflicted lines on the arms of those who are prone to self-harming. Thinking about it a little more I must take a sympathetic point of view. This is an announcement which is something nobody has ever heard before as far as I can remember. I don't think this has come out to any of my psychiatrists, counsellors or friends in the past.

When I was approaching the time of my weak suicide attempt in Manchester I spent a week or two before that sitting alone in my rented room listening to heavy metal bands such as Black Sabbath, Ministry and Megadeth while making small incisions in my forearm. It probably would have been with my sewing scissors, as I wasn't shaving then so it wouldn't have been with a razor blade, and I was sewing plenty of badges on to what was a very recognisable jacket back then. Now it is so recognisable that I get called a legend when I wear it to the Isle of Wight festival.

When I was self-harming in Manchester I would probably have had some alcohol and some cannabis earlier in the evening which, though I didn't realise at that time, was expected to actually make me more depressed not happier according to a study of the biochemistry. I should have seen that from the information under my nose as I had a few basic psychology text books, as I was there to do a BSc in the subject at Manchester Metropolitan University.

In that era I also experimented with LSD, amphetamine, magic mushrooms and ecstasy, but I think I had felt that doing any of these would not be helpful when I came to slashing my wrists in Platt Field Park one night. I can't explain why but something about the hallucinogens really worked for me and so once I had got over the initial fear barrier they became my favourite way to pass each weekend. To start with I feared that if I took too much LSD it might induce a heart attack or more likely an epileptic fit. After finding out that wasn't going to be a side effect I kept taking more and more each time. I became such an Acid head or Tripper that my student friends used to take the piss out of me regarding the subject. Usually it was them saying if they want to have a 'trip' all they needed to do was to become vampires and drink some of my blood as it was so loaded with LSD it would be enough to get them going. One thing I did which I'm not sure if anyone else did was to try and maximise the visual hallucinations - I would take a pair of blotters and put one under each eyelid so the LSD went straight into my eyeballs. I don't know if this actually had any effect but I had convinced myself it did so I was quite happy to sit in a chair sharing spliffs and bottles of drink with other students at house parties after putting a 'trip' under each eyelid and left a few under my tongue. Certainly I did see some unusual sights in those days, as well as having some strange experiences. Some of the best were had in Platt Field Park, as the usual routine was to take whatever drugs we had, be it LSD, Speed or E's in the latter days and then sit around waiting for them to kick in. This would have been me and my mates from first year psychology to start and then as we got established we made friends with the people we shared houses with.

Then once we started feeling the effect we would go for a walk in the park, enjoying the sun fading yet staying nice and warm as it was that time of year. One time we saw a cloud formation drifting over above us which looked identical to the skeleton of a horse formed out of water vapour. Manchester certainly looked just like it does in the introduction of Coronation Street, as there were miles and miles of red brick houses in identical lines which were then full of students, members of the Asian community and people who lives appeared to be just like those in the ITV soap opera watched a couple of times a week. Manchester deserved its reputation for rain and crime as both of these were in abundance. One thing seemed to combine the two as in the bleak midwinter when it was raining felines and canines there was an Ice Cream van that often plied its trade near Maine Road, the old Manchester City football ground. I never confirmed it but the rumour was that in fact it was a cover for a brave drug dealer who had code words such as chocolate for cannabis, Tutti-frutti for Acid and sherbet being cocaine.

There was a married couple who were in their mid-twenties that actually lived in Fallowfield and weren't just staying there while students. The man of the couple met my friends and me as he was also doing the psychology degree, and he introduced us to a lot of the music which was just before our time but he was familiar with, such as Hawkwind, Gong and Steve Hillage. He became like an older brother to us and he had a very caring wife who had obviously accepted the fact that a relationship with him involved a few strange nights now and then and meeting some odd people. For ages he called her 'Gorge' which we used to wonder about till I found out it was an abbreviated version of 'Gorgeous'. Before we had turned up, the two of them had got married in black biking leathers then ridden off to a banquet in a Saxon hall which sounded very romantic and different which appealed to us. I had a group of about five or six regular companions I would go to parties with on Fridays and Saturdays and attend lectures with during the week. Most of them were nineteen years old and had come to university straight from school. I had had a 'gap' year out in the Young Offenders Institution first but only my closest buddies knew that. My group of mates and I had spent many evenings staying up all night tripping, speeding, drifting through reality after a night of consuming Tequila shots at £1 a go then talking till dawn, as I vaguely recall walking back to my flat in the early sunlight of the morning and then sleeping for about ten to twelve hours and so waking up at half six on Sunday evening. This was often very confusing as due to the light levels I didn't know if it was morning or evening as my body clock had been as muddled as my 'Doors of Perception' by my time on acid.

What I did on the night I seriously cut my wrist was have a four-pack of Carlsberg Special Brew to numb the pain, be it physical or emotional. Also I had a few spliffs which I had pre-rolled unusually; to have between the rollies I would have while walking through the park thinking about "life, the universe and everything." As I recall I'd had an essay back which I hoped had done rather well but it hadn't, and so I was becoming more and more convinced this wasn't my subject, and got to a point where I felt rather lonely and jealous of most of my fellow students who had loving, caring partners. Things had really started going downhill when I had moved to a new student's house. I can't remember why I had moved that time as it wasn't my first move, which had been to get out of a house populated with three other 'fresher lads' and a Polish landlady. Nothing against any of the three guys as they did have entertaining tales of growing up in various parts of Leeds and the Midlands. Our landlady provided quite reasonable meals and made the best potato pancakes I think I've ever had when we arrived on time for them. As we made more new friends and discovered Areas of Outstanding Numerous Boozers we missed more and more meals. Another thing which didn't help regarding turning up on time for our half board meals was that next door was a Fish and Chip shop which did fantastic Northern gravy and top quality meat and potato pies which provided an ideal meal in a pastry package.

Looking back on the whole situation now I can see it was probably my destiny that things panned out the way they did. It was like mixing some organic chemicals in an 'A' level chemistry experiment and then sitting back to watch. I knew what was going to happen, it was just a question of how long it would take due to the heat energy and amount of catalyst. The way I see it when I review that part of my life is like this: Having gone to an all-boys boarding school at the age of seven or so after being the only person in the car accident which killed my mum and having no visible cause I stayed at The Old Ride Prep school till I was eleven. Then I started at Plymouth College which only had sixth form girls then; but now in the twenty first century they have girls present and boarding all the way. I boarded for a few years on a weekly basis there at around the age of sixteen. It was probably my dad's survival plan to manage me at the peak of my years of teenage angst, and God was just beginning to enter the equation with some presence at that point as the reason I boarded was that Dad was doing a Diploma in Theology in Bristol on weekdays and then we got back together again on Saturday afternoons. This was when I would say I was going out for a walk and went down to Trefussis Park, which was only five minutes away to have the cigarette for that day as I worked on becoming a nicotine addict despite all the advice from my caring father.

After being the first generation to do them my friends and I scraped through our GCSEs, which I always remember my Uncle calling "the General Collapse of Secondary Education." I went on to do 'A' levels in three of the subjects I had obtained B's in, i.e. the sciences. I probably would have done better doing geography or English rather than physics, but I think because most of my friends were doing physics I did it too, because I thought I could have a laugh with them at the back of the classroom. There were two principal reasons I should have left physics alone and not touched it with a long range telescopic barge pole. The first was that, having done his first degree in engineering, working as an engineering officer in the navy and then teaching maths, shipbuilding, naval architecture and physics at the local further education college, my dad was very good at it and secondly I couldn't do it. I also did general studies which was a chance for us to be told a little about the world we would be going out into in 1990. I was staying at home at that time and I can't deny that Dad was right when we talked it all through afterwards; he said we were like two strangers living in the same house in those days. He was weighing up the possibilities of going off to Africa as a missionary and I was still hoping to be Sir David Attenborough Mark II.

It was at this time of my nurturing that my favourite pastimes when at home over the weekend were playing on my ZX Spectrum or Dad's BBC computer. Then on Saturday evenings I would get dressed up in my New Romantics white shirt, my black leather waistcoat, black jeans and my cowboy boots from Burtons which lasted so well I still had them now, about twenty years later. I also got my left ear pierced and wore gothic earrings portraying skeletons, skulls and black pentagrams. I would go out and meet my friends on the Hoe or the Barbican, and the oldest, or at least the oldest looking of us went in to the local off licence to get a bottle of

Scotsmac or Thunderbirds. They were both aperitifs of about 15% and so very effective at intoxicating teenagers who had probably had a toke or two on a spliff as well. Then a group of three or four of us went down a local backstreet and sat on a wall having swigs of these drinks which tasted hideous but did the job of numbing our feelings, senses and sensibilities while putting our physical control and sense of balance out of order. After about three quarters of an hour we found we had to sit on the ground and lean back against the wall as we'd fall off the wall if we were still sitting on it. It was then I decided I liked sitting on the floor as I couldn't fall off it. We staggered down to Union Street, which I understood had a reputation with many of the world's naval forces as a place for cheap alcohol and women. My best friends and I went to an alternative/independent music club 'Connections' where they played things like Jane's Addiction, Ministry, Sisters of Mercy and Primus.

We would have enough hard cash to buy a few drinks throughout the night which finished at two o'clock in those days, when people smoked in clubs rather than hanging round near doorways as they do these days. I don't know how these things become officially recognised but I'm keen to introduce 'cloud of smokers' as a collective noun, on the same level as 'superfluity of nuns'. We would soon find we'd spent all our money, including that which had been supposed to pay for a taxi to get us home rather than leave us with a cold, wet stagger home which could last for hours. Just a detail for anyone who doesn't know; Plymouth is one of those cities which, like Rome, is very familiar with contours, not being pancake flat like Manchester. However being in the club and still able to consume alcohol we then began an activity we called Minesweeping. This was the process of standing inconspicuously leaning against a pillar while watching some of the other clubbers, clearly more interested in a night's dancing and getting off with a girl than achieving sensory obliteration. They would see a girl in an appealing outfit such as a thin summer dress and clearly very little if anything underneath. They walked towards the dance floor and put their two thirds full pint of Strongbow cider on the free standing shelving with chrome struts. Then as soon as they moved towards the present apple of their eye we came up behind them to relieve them of a responsibility. I don't know if it's got a different name in non-coastal cities such as road-sweeping but when I look out of my current flat widow and see one of the MCMVs such as HMS Grimsby I can't think Mine Counter Measure Vessel without having a 'Connections Nightclub' flashback. Being able to look out of my flat window and see navy ships going up and down the River Tamar is one of my favourite things about the place. Being into devious things, I've always been particularly keen on submarines and I did enjoy watching a U-boat go down the river the other year. I've also seen the monstrous HMS Vanguard and one of my favourite films is 'Das Boot.'

Doing my time at Plymouth College following The Old Ride I was still on a fairly tight rein despite having a few fairly free running weekends. Following that directly with eighteen months in a YOI basically meant that for the majority of ten years I had been pretty controlled, so following that with a stay in Manchester in the early nineties and giving me a student grant back then and introducing me to a crowd who were fairly keen to party in a city that provided all we required for that. During my year living the wrong side of Moss side and then in Fallowfield I went to gigs of Ministry, Ozric Tentacles, and Pitchshifter, then went to Glastonbury for the first time which started a definite trend as since then I've been there three times since, once each to Reading and Leeds and to the Isle of Wight seven times thanks to David Bowie. It's his fault, because I saw him perform at Glastonbury and had to see him again as it was such a good show, and so as he was at the Isle of Wight the next year I went there. Finding the Isle was a gear down on Glasters having everyone well chilled out and not being anything like as commerce centred. Thanks to the jacket I started working on in Manchester and which now has about one hundred and fifty badges on which results in other festival goers recognising it from previous years and calling me a legend. Also, I've been photographed by local press and a lady from New York and one year I was interviewed by Channel 4 people connected to 'Big Brother.' At the time I was somewhat intoxicated and so gave my true opinion of the show. I told then I thought it was rubbish saying when I watch TV I want to see real actors not just ordinary people similar to those I can see if I take a walk in to town. Another reason I like the Isle of Wight is that I have found my grandparents and Dad lived there when Grandad was working for the navy in Portsmouth.

Returning to the Manchester breakdown, I left the Polish landlady's residence and had a few various digs and ended up in a house which had three girls and me in. I hadn't known who I would be sharing it with when I moved in and probably wouldn't have selected that one if I had known. Half the time they were out with boyfriends and the other half had girl nights in. The details I remember are the bathroom nearly always been used but smelling lovely when I did get to use it, and most weekends I could hear sounds of sexual pleasure coming from at least one of the bedrooms despite having the radio on in my room as it was a modern house with tiresomely thin walls. One night it all became too much following a few weeks cutting enough lines in my arms for it to be mistaken for an intricate street map; I decided to finish it all and so had my cans of Special Brew and then walked to Platt Fields and sat in the pavilion with a razor blade. Having not researched the topic there were two important things which I'm now glad I didn't know then. Namely that it's best to be in a hot bath to kill oneself by wrist slashing and also that it's advised that you cut along your arms not across. I sat on the park's bench and debated with myself which arm to do first. Being right handed I decided to do that arm first as it being my stronger arm I guessed I could use that one better once it was damaged and so then cut my left. However after making a deep cut right across the right arm it hurt trying to hold the razor blade in that hand and so I was left fainting in the park in the middle of the night bleeding profusely from my right forearm.

I woke up at about six in the morning in a pool of cold, sticky blood with a hangover and a rather unfamiliar problem to deal with. Not wanting to phone an ambulance or stagger to the nearest hospital I chose to phone my nearest friend in Manchester. A top guy called Clive who was just about my soul mate and I knew he'd do me a favour so I phoned him. I can't remember quite what I said there and then but I remember next he and a small group of other friends turned up shortly after. They knew me well enough to understand why I was very reluctant to go to hospital. I'd dealt with mental health people in Plymouth's infamous Moorhaven and then HMP Exeter, Portland YOI and outpatient sessions with a 'trick cyclist' before moving to Manchester.

One of my friends was so eager to help me that he offered to put some stitches into my arm himself. However as it worked out, about half of them said I should go to the hospital and half said I should just do whatever made me feel comfortable. In conclusion I decided I needed a few sutures and though I was very grateful to my friend for offering to do it all in all I felt it would be better to have a qualified nurse do the job. I can't remember how we got from the park to the nearest A and E as I don't think any of us had a car, I wasn't up to walking any distance and taxi drivers were rather careful regarding getting bodily fluids on their upholstery.

Whatever we did I was in a cubicle being sewn up before long and I planned to leave as soon as possible after that. However, when a mental health nurse came and started asking me questions about how I had got such a cut on my arm it soon became clear to the kindly, friendly nurse that I was going to have to leave the A and E department and take up a bed in a different ward. Now I think that was when I started wondering about it, but at some stage in my psychological history I wondered why all the serious mental health hospitals are built of red bricks. Admittedly, most buildings in Manchester are made from red brick but Moorhaven should have been granite like HMP Dartmoor, but it was red brick. I know these days a lot of thought goes into considering colour schemes for hospitals, schools and prisons so I'm inclined to believe red is seen as a good homely, nurturing colour, reminiscent of womb experiences and so it is considered to make a good colour scheme for psychiatric wards.

In the past I had been cooperative and non-resistant when being retained or restrained, be it in assorted boarding schools, a YOI or in a hospital with the aim of partaking in any required medical activities. I'm thinking principally of having EEGs to read my brain waves, occasions when I've been in a scanning machine using an enormous electro-magnet and previous stitch ups including getting a few in the back from Dr Payne when I stayed over a weekend with S.P. as I said earlier. However this time I was being a bit more resistant to being contained, and this was when I started to receive Cognitive Therapy. I was in a psychiatric unit in Didsbury and I found it so frustrating that I chose to break out of it. I did so by taking a knife from the canteen and using it as a screwdriver to undo the catch on my bedroom window which prevented it opening more than a couple of centimetres. However once out on the streets I didn't have any people to go and see, as it was in the holidays so all my friends had gone home to see their families. Thus I went back to the house I was still renting a room in and it didn't take long for the police to come and find me there.

It ended up with me being picked up by my dad who took me back to Plymouth and installed me there at the new psychiatric unit which replaced Moorhaven. This one had the pleasant, relaxing name Glenbourne as these places do. However inside there were and still are three wards in which people are treated for addictions, personality problems, schizophrenia and bi-polar disorder among other things. They may have sussed security regarding people entering and leaving but what they had no control over was what visitors brought in to give the inmates, or clients, as they wanted to call us. I know this for two main reasons, one was what I managed to do and the other was a guy in the same ward but sharing a dormitory with a couple of others. I confess I had a friend of mine who was a drug dealer come in and make deliveries to me on his motorbike. As we could smoke in the TV lounge back then what I used to do with guys there who had been to HMP Exeter or similar was engage in this type of conversation.

"It makes sense that they don't mind people having spliffs in prison when you think about it." I started off.

"Of course it does when you look at why," came back a reply from Smoky Joe.

"It's why they're OK with puff but don't like the other drugs; speed, coke, E's etc."

"Yes. Have a smoke and you'll be chilled out and so won't want a riot or anything like that. However the others give you extra energy and make people aggressive." He explained.

"Well I remember once I was at Portland and a guard opened the door when I wasn't expecting anyone to come in so I'd just had my spliff. He looked at me and said 'Open the window. I'll be back in ten minutes'. So I did and so when he came round with the Prison Chaplain my cell didn't smell of hash. The guards are happy if you get stoned rather than piss them off."

"I'd love a spliff here just to help me stop getting wound up by the routine and the fact I'm not getting any visits."

Once I heard that I'd let him know I had some being regularly delivered and he could buy some off me if he wanted. When I'd done that I found he was mates with another guy there who was having bottles of Smirnoff vodka poured into empty Evian water bottles and brought in by his girlfriend. These are some of the reasons that having Christmas in the local Bedlam wasn't half as bad as I thought it would be.

Chapter 20

I think one thing I need to explain would be a matter regarding my disbelief. I reckon generally if I'm told something and it comes from what I judge to be a reliable supply of information I'll accept it as being true. This probably isn't a particularly good way to go about treating information and supplies of data but it usually seems to help me tell the credible from the incredible or unbelievable.

However one type of information supply seems to be employed to be economical with the truth and tell tall tales about its subjects. What I'm talking about here is the way when I'm watching the news, regardless of which channel is on, we are told of a teenager who was the victim of a horrific car accident, the injured party of a gang drive-by shooting or unlucky enough to be a casualty of the latest terrorist suicide bombing. There is no denying that these people didn't deserve what happened to them, they didn't ask for it or invite it, but as I've known since I was five, life is very unfair and unjust.

What I am denying and I don't find at all credible is that this only happens to the children who are little angels, who wouldn't hurt a fly even if the entire human civilisation depended on it and never said a word to upset or aggravate their siblings, parents and classmates. Not very long ago I read *"The Lovely Bones"* by Alice Sebold about Susie

Salmon but I haven't seen the film. One thing that makes it a good book once you get into it - which most people I asked about it said you need to give it a chapter or two to get up and running - but once you're in she looks down on the real world with real believable sensible interactions. If most teenagers who are killed in a way that wasn't their fault and they as the victims looked down on the news report about them and then heard their elegy I think they would wonder whose funeral they were at. On the whole these days teenagers don't get on with the elderly people of their street like devoted friends, as they often hang out in groups on the corners and ask the ones who look weak willed to go and get them a pack of twenty Mayfair from the illegal immigrants shop, and if they've got the cash ask for a bottle of White Lightening chemical cider which is 7.5% and has only been near an apple when its delivery lorry passed an orchard going along the motorway.

Another mysterious thing connected to teenagers of this day and age is how on earth do they manage to get through so many condoms considering the number of empty packets and used prophylactic bits of kit I find lying around in the streets. But I bet if I went up to any of my local lads and lasses and accused them of littering the proximity with prophylaxes they would not have a clue what I was on about, and knowing their behaviour if they applied 'the little grey cells' with a process of elimination they would conclude it was a word for fag butt or dogend.

One of my current friends has the nickname Dogend. Nicknames are often prescribed to people to make fun of a characteristic or trait they have. Sometimes they mock something which individuals are stuck with, be it a surname or a physical feature. For example when I was a school boy with the surname Bridgwater I confess my nickname used to fluctuate between Bogwater and Bilgewater, although it should have been Bilgwater if its users could spell correctly. Still, my friend Dogend is so called because he smokes like the proverbial trooper, and having a limited budget at times he needs to go out and trawl the streets for butts left lining the pavement. At first I guessed there wasn't a science to 'buttology' but now I think there is. For a start, collecting dogends is a very temporally influenced pastime as weather plays a major role. Seasons and time of day feature and clearly so does geography. Winter is generally a bad period due to increased moisture levels and time of day causes fluctuation in visibility levels. Geography is greatly influenced by local features, with bus shelters being far more favourable than bus stops as the area of cover keep the ends dry and so reusable as they are, or at least ready to be broken down and then reassembled. One good thing about the law stating smokers must leave the building for a nicotine intake is that people like him now know where to go to find the piles of cigarette ends at pub doors, office blocks and particularly those who establish sand boxes for ends to be left in. Such can be visited in case of emergency, so then we are very grateful to the city council, the Eagle pub and Morrison's supermarket as they all have provided buckets of sand at their entrances from which dogends can be harvested.

Years ago I first heard of the 'butterfly effect' but nowadays I think I've discovered the 'dogend effect'. If I have an adequate supply of tobacco in my pocket and so I'm not trawling the gutters for ends I can be sure that then there will be plenty of them visible and available. Also the weather will be dry so they can be found any and everywhere. However as soon as I smoke my last one and take my daily walk I can be certain the usable ends will be as common as Nobel literature prize winners. There will also have been a shower so they are all sopping wet and completely useless anyway.

I have been living in my current flat for numerous years and apart from about five days, I've gone for a walk every day I spend the night there. I was usually greeted when I returned to it by Alice if she wasn't asleep on the window sill absorbing sunshine. She and quite a few other cats I've known have a lot in common with a campervan which used to park along the road from my dad's house. That had the name on the back 'auto sleeper' which describes a lot of cats. I wish I could control my sleep patterns as well as they can but I regularly wake up two or three times in the night and that's what I expect these days. Ever since my teenage years at home I've always been more comfortable going to sleep with a radio or a tape providing some background noise. Habitually I go for Radio 4 which switches to and from the World Service during the small hours. Just in case something comes on which I don't want to hear about or I'm bored of hearing over and over again, as often happens around the time of American Presidential elections, I've a choice of about ten tapes with my bedtime stories on. These include the radio version of *Hitchhikers Guide to the Galaxy* in the original box with Don't Panic in big bold letters on the box. Also various famous actors reading *Dracula, Frankenstein, Don Quixote, Captain Beaky, Fall of the House of Usher* and *The Dunwich Horror.*

It's very much an individual thing relating to the one in question as to whether or not I'm with a cat I can share my bed with. My companion for years as I went from infancy to latter teenage years was Brum and she was a cat I slept with every night as I've mentioned. Alice is impossible to bed down with though as she always wakes me up with a face full of whiskers and feline halitosis. I think a walrus in the face would be a similar experience, and one I can do without first thing in the morning. Referring to nicknames again, I gave Alice the name Squeak. This is because she was a small cat with a very small, quiet voice. I don't know but I think it may be due to an incident in her kittenhood. When she was a smaller ball of fluff she had a disagreement with an ailurophobic born again Christian. It resulted in her being kicked and losing sight in her right eye. I don't know if it's possible but I think her vocal cords may have been damaged too as sometimes she opened her mouth but no sound came out. When a sound did emit it was always a plaintive bleaty, mewy squeak.

She did have a strong personality which she could convey quite adeptly. When I come in the flat I have to go up four flights of steps to reach my landing level. On two of these she could meet me but the standard routine was to be looking down at me from the top of the stairs and then come halfway down to get on a level with my face. Thanks to Lewis Carroll I invented an alternative nickname for Alice due to her doing this. Galumph is listed in the dictionary as being a word coined by Carroll, and so as Alice was a small cat I called her a 'galumphling' when she bounced down the stairs to see what I had in the shopping bags.

I remember when I was in my mid teenage years the Burmese cat we had then called Brum showed me a really strong display of determination which did indeed touch me to the heart. Dad and I came back home one afternoon and she was sitting in the front garden as she often did. However when it was time to go in we quickly saw she couldn't use her back legs and they were paralysed for some reason. We immediately took her to the vet and were told she a nasty bruise at the base of her spine which may have been caused by a hit from a vehicle or possibly it came from a kick. Yet her legs should be usable again when the swelling went down. When we got her home she was given a comfortable place to sit on the sofa and we left her there when we went upstairs to bed, not wanting to wake her up or cause her pain by putting any pressure on the bruise. After I had been lying in bed listening to 'Book at Bedtime' I heard a noise from the stairway and so I got up and went to see what was causing it. I found my lovely little cat had pulled herself off the sofa, across part of the floor and was now hauling herself up the stairs using just her front legs as she always shared my bed and that was such a habit she didn't want an injury to stop her doing so. Therefore to keep her happy I got the duvet off my bed and slept with her on the sofa till her back legs were working properly again which took about a week.

Having been an only child often with only a pet for company, I'm more than familiar with talking to myself or my furry friend. I did have a couple of rats as pets for a while in my previous flat and they were named Pollux and Castor after the two Gemini twins as that is my star sign.

Chapter 21

As I've mentioned, having a three year criminal sentence at the age of eighteen and a criminal record for the rest of my life which could well be linked to some extent to having seen my mum killed in a car accident with no explanation and so no understanding by me is a major invisible burden. Every job I've ever applied for asks the usual relevant questions regarding qualifications, experience and the blank page in which I get to describe myself, my habits and why I think I'm the one for the position on offer. However what I discovered years ago is that whether you're applying to be a cemetery maintenance assistant (grave digger), a teaching assistant or a volunteer with your local group of helpful community workers in somewhere such as Keyham Community Partnership, people will ask about your criminal record. I was even asked about it when I thought about going on The Weakest Link. However they all send paperwork saying that they will not discriminate regarding sexuality, gender, race, belief or age. What they don't say they won't use as a discrimination influence is criminal history.

The one time I really had an issue with this was when I felt ready to do my degree in Literary Studies with Theology and Philosophy at the College of St. Mark and St. John. (Marjons). I assumed by their Christian name that they would be aware of things such as forgiveness, especially as it had happened ten years previously and wasn't against them. Also my dad had done his MA in Applied Theology at the same place, so some of the staff in the relevant department knew him and he would stand up for me. However, I applied with full honesty and after a long wait over the summer I was told that I was seen as an unsuitable applicant for such a position as a student in the college. This infuriated me and my dad to such an extent that we made an appeal for the decision to be reconsidered. Apparently as a nation, we the English are particularly poor when it comes to complaining and standing up for our rights so this was a major project to take on. It resulted in us going to a meeting with the Vice-Chancellor, Head of Student Services and someone from the English department if I remember rightly. We did eventually convince them that I wasn't a psychotic criminal having been given a three years sentence when I was eighteen, having a psychiatric breakdown in Manchester partly due to LSD and having been on anti-depressants for a period of time since then. It was unintentional, but what made me suffer was that I was told I could join the student body a week after the course had begun. So everyone else had met each other and gone to fresher's activities and begun making friendships. Therefore I was always slightly off kilter with everyone and being twenty seven while most others were nineteen having either gone straight from school to college or at best having had a gap year out.

To try and get a friendship or two with some students at the college I got involved with a bit of theatre, as at school I had been in the Christmas review show, a Shakespeare performance and the updated Pilgrim's Progress. As the review show was in the 80's and the scenes were written relating to things popular at the time I played Murdoch from the A Team which was top of the TV charts back then. In our Shakespeare which we did for GCSE I played the French Duke of Orleans in King Henry the Fifth. I must admit that back at the start of GCSE the name Shakespeare had a quite negative effect on me and my classmates. Quite a few still felt unimpressed by the end of the course, but I found that getting up on stage and bringing it to life showed me the energy of the script. Especially with the quality of the lead role performed by my class mate John Lambert and directed by my Deputy House Master Mr Hunter. Unfortunately all the good speeches were those of Harry so being a Frenchman I didn't get to hear them except in the rehearsals. I particularly liked the one outside Harfleur.

Once more unto the breach, dear friends, once more;
Or close the wall up with our English dead!
In peace there's nothing so becomes a man
As modest stillness and humility:
But when the blast of war blows in our ears,
Then imitate the action of the tiger:
Stiffen the sinews, summon up the blood,
Disguise fair nature with hard-favoured rage;
Then lend the eye a terrible aspect.

Since then I've become so keen on Shakespearian plays one of my ambitions is to see everyone is some form, be it on TV, in a theatre or what I really enjoy which is in the grounds of a stately home. So far in that line I've seen Twelfth Night at Mount Edgecombe and Love's Labour's Lost at Cotehele. In the same manner another performance I especially enjoyed was The Turning of The Screw opera by Benjamin Britten in Prideaux Place with a chamber orchestra under the stairs and the singers using the main staircase and hallway to act in. Thanks to the music and an eerie atmosphere it really was quite scary.

While I was at Marjons a notice caught my eye which said the drama department wanted to do a play for the end of the year and so anyone interested in performing or working backstage should put their name down. I did and when it came to fruition I found I was the only person not doing a BA in Drama Studies to be involved. I think this was foolish of the others doing Literary Studies, as in our Modern Drama module we looked at Bertolt Brecht, focusing on *Mother Courage* while the drama department and I presented *The Good Person of Szechwan* which was another piece of 'epic theatre'. They both illustrated his theory of drama which he chose to expound in his *Little Treatise on the Theatre* saying he discarded the idea that drama should seek to create the illusion of reality. This was clear from the very start of The Good Woman as it started with me and a couple of others playing Chinese Gods looking down on the mortal world.

As I had spent about eighteen months doing door to door sales before I started my degree I was interested in looking at Miller's *Death of a Salesman*. I had hated the job as it had no basic rate of pay, it was all commission based so no sales equalled no income. In parts I felt the same as I thought Willie Loman did.

"Willy Loman never made a lot of money. His name was never in the paper. He's not the finest character that ever lived. But he's a human being, and a terrible thing is happening to him. So attention must be paid."

In our studies we went on from 'epic theatre' to 'Theatre of the Absurd' in which we looked at *Happy Days* and *Waiting for Godot* by Beckett and *The Birthday Party* by Pinter. I can't say what it is but something about the work of Harold Pinter seemed to be on my wavelength. He may have planted the seed of the idea of confessing in my mind as near the end of *The Birthday Party* Mr McCann and Mr Goldberg tell Lulu that it would be a good thing for her to make a confession.

One thing I found especially frustrating around that time was our lecturer and the textbooks we used regularly mentioned Edward Albee and his work *Who's afraid of Virginia Woolf?* Somebody had stolen the DVD of it from the college library. Whenever Tennessee Williams and *A Streetcar named Desire* or *Cat on a Hot Tin Roof* got mentioned we could watch the library copy and so see its significance. Eventually years later the Plymouth City library got a DVD of the classic Elizabeth Taylor, Richard Burton version of Albee's play so I have seen it but still want to see it live. I knew that DVD would be very entertaining as shortly before then I had seen the Burton/Taylor performance of *The Taming of the Shrew* in which there was just about tangible electricity between the two of them. Initially it was just like mild static but by the end it equated lightening of tens of thousands of amps.

Also to try and improve my chance for socialising I looked into the possibility of establishing a Bridge club as I had been taught this wonderful game, poker and many other games by my great aunt who had a huge mouthful of a name and so for convenience was known as Miss V de K due to her Dutch surname. She was an incredible character as she was a real 'horsey woman' like Princess Anne and she had great stories from the war. Particularly from her youth in which she had been involved in driving ambulances round during the Blitz and she had very memorable stories of seeing Plymouth's Union Street in flames. These days it is still a site for hot action, but of a very different kind. Afterwards she got to almost Olympic standard with her dressage riding and went on to become a known teacher of the subject right across the West Country. She had lived in a Manor House for as long as I could remember and it was the most incredible place I ever used to stay at. The house was in two parts; the 'upstairs' half where the residents lived which was composed of numerous master bedrooms, a morning room, an enormous dining room which was only used about once a year and that was never to full capacity to my knowledge. There was also a living room which was so huge I could fit my entire present flat in the room. In most rooms of this half I used to wonder how the light bulbs were changed as the ceilings were so high up. A Brobdingnagian hallway had a fireplace which was so big it had a barrier built round it with brass railings and a seat on top of that which could be sat on by about ten individuals. There was a chest of drawers loaded with curios and mysterious objects in the corner which was where I first saw an ostrich egg, an elephants tooth and a poniard type item which was formed of a wavy steel blade inscribed with a snake. It also contained compartments of insects, butterflies and all the most peculiar examples of life which could be collected and stored by a gentleman.

Then there was the 'downstairs' half which consisted of the biggest kitchen I ever been familiar with which linked to separate rooms such as a pantry, a dairy, a store room and a scullery. Then there was the second staircase which was like a seaside donkey against a thoroughbred racehorse compared to the main stairway. There was also a wing for all the servants to live in, not that there had ever been any in the time I remembered. It was so built into the house to operate in such a way that the main rooms had buttons built into the walls so they could be pressed to ring a bell in the servant's quarters. It was just like the one Mr Hudson responded to in *Upstairs, downstairs*. Back then as a teenager I was fascinated by ghosts, werewolves and vampires, reading the classics such as Shelley, Stoker and lesser known ones such as Poe, James and Le Fanu. This Manor house was just the kind of place I imagined when I read about haunted houses or Borley Rectory which was supposed to be the most haunted house in England. One cold, dark, wet and windy night I was staying the night in a room at the end of a corridor and so well away from any human company. I was kept awake by the howling gale and the sound of a branch tapping on the window. Not that I knew it then it was a reproduction of the scene with Mr Lockwood in *Wuthering Heights* which since then has become a book I have now read and enjoyed rereading by candlelight. However I looked at the window and thought I heard an inhuman cry and was greeted by a strange, eerie face looking in at me. It struck fear to my heart and so I leapt out of bed and ran down the corridor to find someone to give me some support. The adults had not bedded down yet so I had to go down the main staircase and get to the giant living room which I managed eventually. I burst in and became the centre of much amusement once I described my problems, as it was known there was a barn owl on the premises who had a bizarre voice and could look like a human face in the roughest weather conditions especially if one had phantoms, spectres and things that go bump in the night on the mind.

The grounds were quite beyond my comprehension back then too, as I was in my mid-teens when I was most familiar with the place. There was a drive of about one hundred metres which was lined with rhododendrons and had an island of camellias with roadway on each side. This led up to the most impressive front door I think I've ever opened, though we usually parked in the courtyard and went in the back door to the kitchen. The courtyard was phenomenal as well as it had a one man forge where the local farrier could work the horse shoes of the animals which resided in the stables, which were just through the woods towards some of the fields - all still part of the Manor grounds. There were also numerous store rooms and outhouses which were populated by members of the cat community. These were in two groups; the 'house' cats and the 'outdoor' cats. Members of the 'outdoor' bunch never came in the house but could go anywhere else they wanted and were given food *in situ* at the stables tack room and left to keep the rodents out of the hay bales. They numbered around twenty or so and were generally left to regulate their own population and health.

Then the 'house' cats were better known characters fed in the kitchen such as Charlie the King of the Realm. He was a ginger and white beast who was so obese he could pass as a modern teenager and he had a cyst the size of a ping-pong ball. He would stand up against Heidi the resident Alsatian without a worry, and he was famous for his appetite. Once he had come across a plate with raw spaghetti on and under a cover but with the ends protruding. He had apparently chewed off the extending tips trimming them back to the edges of the cover. He was also known to kill and eat a number of rabbits on a regular basis. Also there was Tinker who was a cute little black ball of energy who was very friendly but not a good friend to have on one's lap as she had the sharpest little needles in her paws that I've ever come across. Of course being a loving little female she enjoyed doing the kneading which kittens do to stimulate their mother's milk which was dangerous to any trousers and thus knees and thigh flesh.

It was the most successful house I have known without a television and a place where I did a considerable amount of reading and discussing issue of all aspects of the world. I was taught much about the reading and writing of poetry being introduced to *Old Possum's Book of Practical Cats*. There were so many individuals in the book such as Mr Mistoffelees, The Rum Tum Tugger, Growltiger and Macavity: The Mystery Cat. Then there are cats I've known in my childhood which I could write poems about such as Tabatha, Brum, Ting and Rags.

However I couldn't establish a link with anyone at college on anything even approaching the level of dedication and devotion I had encountered with the cats, particularly Brum trying to ascend the stairs to sleep with me. What I probably should have done is set up a writing group as having done that since then I've managed to meet groups of people who enjoy writing as I do and so we encourage each other and give support and reassurance to each other. I certainly had creative juices beyond the academic area in those days, as it was a combination of English and philosophical studies which prompted me to write the follow piece of verse. How I was to discover the word Hippopotomonstrosesquipedaliophobia I can't remember, but I was very amused that such a word should mean fear of long words so I felt obliged to do something with it. I've been praised for the piece of writing by members of Plymouth Proprietary Library writing group and also the poets at Plymouth Arts Centre Language club.

Hippopotomonstrosesquipedaliophobia

Frankenstein and Wittgenstein; two monsters, different kinds.
Shelley's monster is OK, but Ludwig does blow minds.
Tractatus Logico-Philosophicus, cool name for a book,
Yet given choice I'd not give the text a second look.

Still Wittgenstein's not just to blame, one member of a bunch.
Transcendentalism must make great chat over lunch.
Then after that it's fruit, ice-cream or try some cheese,
The fatal hemlock leave alone, unlike silly Socrates.

Categorical Imperatives make sense to old Herr Kant,
To me he's just a German who does no more than rant.
Kierkegaard and Nietzsche, then Heidegger and friends.
Each one sends me round metaphysical type bends.

Paradox and fallacy, Professor loves them all,
He solves them at the speed of light, I do a mental crawl.

Cogito ergo sum: I think therefore I am!

But what I think is that I am out thought by cold wet Spam.

In another attempt to try and get involved with the students around me back then I became a member of the student-staff council representing the English department for a year. Even this didn't manage to intimately connect me with any members of the department, so I ended up still associating with my previous friends who were nearly all experienced drug takers, drinkers or regulars at the local psychiatric clinics or prisons.

Thus, after a year of my student life, I considered myself to just about be an alcoholic and so felt the need to go through rehab. It was arranged for me to attend a treatment centre, and so I explained the situation to the college. Having gone to the trouble of taking me on they decided to stick with me and so I was given a year out to dry up and get back on the rails. This resulted in me being in a residential clinic on 9/11 2001 which gave me a very strong memory. It is the most recent time I remember watching TV and it inducing my shedding of tears. The film from the Twin Towers was being broadcast live and a crowd of us were in the TV lounge seeing the unfortunate Americans jumping out of the doomed structures just before they came crashing to the ground. I couldn't believe how it got to me but I supposed quite a few things had happened there to get me quite emotionally stirred up. Another strong memory I have from the same place was one evening when I was talking to a guy who had just been there for a couple of days when I'd been there for weeks so I was explaining the routine to him. I had to tell him about when we got our medications be they for epilepsy, withdrawal symptoms or anything else. He said he needed treatment for HIV. I told him my epileptic history so he paid me back by giving me his HIV history.

He had been a heroin addict for a considerable length of time and so had flogged all his possessions to raise cash for the next hit. Like most he had become a criminal to maintain his supply and eventually he robbed some cash off someone who had known him intimately for years. They had counted on him not letting them down and so when he did they felt obliged to take revenge. What he then told me makes me cringe when I think of it now and I'm very tempted to call it pure evil. His 'friend' had a hit for himself but he agreed to share it so as to restore their friendship. So his friend used the syringe and passed it to the guy I was talking to then. He was forced to use the same syringe to get the second half of the hit. He was given the needle by the other who knew he had HIV himself and so he could be pretty sure he was passing on the infection and he did. It would be a very slow, drawn out death, but really it was murdering the guy who I was talking to in the clinic then. I was impressed by my companion's moral strength as he accepted the situation and never tried to get his own back and didn't seem to be bitter at all.

While I was there having a good revaluation of my life I considered a number of things which I had either ignored or just put off dealing with till they seemed significant. One of these was God who came sharply into focus with the third of twelve steps which said, 'Make a decision to turn our will and our lives over to the care of God as we understand him.' Now, as some readers will know, all Alcoholics or Narcotics Anonymous meetings have the serenity prayer. These days I use it in my local church when I do the intercessional prayers once every few Sundays as my finishing point. I use it as a reminder to me of all the suffering I have witnessed and endured myself caused by drugs and drink. This is the point at which I'll confess that even having been through rehab I don't feel I can control my drinking one hundred per cent. This is why when I take Communion I only have the bread and leave the wine. What I mean by not totally controlling it is I can think of quite a few occasions which still repeat fairly regularly when I'm with friends of mine and I want to go home. However if they pour out a drink for me I can't leave it or say not to, so I can't leave when I want to and that is often on a Saturday night. Plenty of times I've planned to go to church at eleven on Sunday morning but, not having left a friend's house till about four in the morning having had beers, more than a bottle of red wine and some brandies, I can't make it.

The Serenity Prayer

God grant me the serenity to accept the things I cannot change,

Courage to change the things I can,

And the wisdom to know the difference.

Since then I have discovered it in a number of places I did not expect to find it including on a locket hanging between the breasts of Montana Wildhack, right near the end of Kurt Vonnegut's novel *Slaughterhouse Five*. Still, who knows what to expect when on the planet Tralfamadore. I know I don't.

Chapter 22

I'm not a serious student of fashion, be it present, current styles and trends or the history of the subject. Basically my history regarding clothing goes as follows. From about seven to twenty I had to wear a uniform most of the time. At The Old Ride Preparatory school we all wore grey corduroy shorts, grey shirts and grey knee length socks which had maroon decoration. The school also provided particular maroon belts with snake buckles and purple elastic to make garters out of. This was all polished off with a smart maroon blazer trimmed with gold piping cord all around the edges. Unlike a considerable number of prep schools, including some famous ones, we didn't have caps or boaters. One reason I was glad I didn't go to Plymouth College Preparatory school before joining the Main School was that they had to wear caps of green, red and black stripes. I didn't mind the colour scheme, in fact most of my time in Main School I chose to wear a deck chair blazer. Once I was in the sixth form and it was permissible I wore a blue blazer with pale grey trousers. It was quite similar to the blazers worn by men who had been in various organisations which are identifiable by nice impressive badges on the blazer breast pockets, which was something our blazers lacked.

Plymouth College, or PMC as it was known in history as that stood for Plymouth and Mannamead College which was its proper title, had the most recognisable uniform in the city if not the whole county. The ironic thing was we weren't obliged to wear that, we could were a dark grey suit and display the easily identified colours on a tie. The unmissable colours of the blazer were stripes of green, red and black in the same tones as those colours on a snooker table and in such wide lines we were accused of being walking deck chairs.

Being in an all-male environment the majority of that time I didn't think about clothing as a way of attracting female interest, and I wasn't buying it myself then anyway. I could pretty much choose what I would like as long as it came from C and A, George's at Asda or St. Michael's at Marks and Sparks. I suppose my first real adventure in to the world of a trendy dress sense happened during the summer of a year in the late eighties, where I saw plenty of tie-dyed garments and was now old enough to be aware of Woodstock. I saw the Woodstock documentary film which had won an Oscar and found I enjoyed the music of the scene. Little of that kind of thing was in the present charts, but in the back of my dad's record cabinet behind Abba, Simon and Garfunkel and Neil Diamond - which were behind the classical such as Beethoven symphonies, Mozart Horn concertos - could be found Joan Baez, Joe Cocker and Canned Heat.

The people on stage at Woodstock and those in the audience that had any clothes on had a lot of tie-dyed material and I confess that appealed to me, so I decided to produce some myself and before too long I had expanded that to some basic batik work as well. A little bit of marking out words and simple shapes using bleach straight from the nozzle of a toilet Duck added some possibilities. Thus I developed a taste for garments which were individual and unique. This probably explained why I had enjoyed and preferred a technicoloured blazer at school. It was the choice of the minority, and that is usually my preference. I can't remember when, but it was my preferring to be the black sheep and so be recognised which eventually led to me writing this piece.

Me vs. Them

Everybody has a curse: smoking, drinking, maybe worse.
Yet mine I find is quite unique, it makes me feel a shopping freak.
Charity shops are just too much; they use a cause, good value touch.

I need no new glass candlesticks; I just need an Oxfam fix.
Yet Scope and Help the Aged can make me revise my shopping plan.
The PDSA tag works for me, more than GAP or Versace.

A designer label says to me the wearer lacks personality,
They're just all mindless senseless sheep, in with the flock they need to keep.
F.C.U.K. worst of the lot. Can't they spell fuck, it does seem not.

The last few years it seems to me, extreme loss of individuality.
To stand out scares you all to hell, that Burberry check you think works well
Old suitcase lining may suit you. The idea of difference will not do.

Over the last years I seem to have been witnessing people's individuality fading away with two particular examples really being trying. The first has been an unfortunate trend in 'body art' which I think may have been started around the time of the Spice Girls introducing Girl Power. I won't try and put a date to it as usually when I look back to something and try to date it I find more time has passed than I expect or realise. I think certain things were a couple of years ago but find they are between five and ten years. I suppose everybody and everything is time travelling, just without any control over it and always in the same direction. I've seen documentaries on TV with top scientists from Oxbridge and the Ivy League and currently I'm led to believe time travel is fundamentally viable, just the amount of energy it would require is the problem. As and when we master nuclear fusion it will give a major jump in the right direction along the road equating to the "yellow brick road" with "The Emerald City" matching up with achievable temporal transportation.

I don't know who the first celebrity to have a very noticeable tattoo at the base of their spine, at a level which meant that it was particularly noticeable when the lady in question was wearing hipster jeans and a top which revealed the majority of their midriff. However it certainly began a major trend of tattoos of intricate Celtic designs over people's lumbar vertebrae, round their arms and then to be different on the base of their necks. Women became keener and keener to receive and display dermis decorations such as butterflies, swallows, hearts and children's birth dates. These would be on various body parts depending on how often they wished to display them and to whom. It was common to have them on ankles which are acceptably displayed in public in this day and age, in contrast to ankles one hundred years earlier or so in the late Victorian, early Edwardian era. Then a flash of an ankle could bring a lady's reputation crashing down faster than she'd be bundled off to a site such as 'St

Aubyn's home for immoral women and girls of failed chastity' which was linked to a nunnery such as the one Prince Hamlet was thinking of when he told Ophelia to get to it.

Chapter 23

Done up in my Ray-ban style shades, dark suit, Trilby hat and full length SS officer black leather coat I was sure all the police and airport security guards that looked at me must have thought I was a throwback to the Cold War. I had enjoyed reading lots of John le Carré novels and, like most patriotic British individuals, I had always been a fan of Commander James Bond, Royal Navy.

I'd forgotten just how much fun flying could be, having been on terra firma for the last twenty years apart from ferry trips taken annually to the Isle of Wight for the fantastic music festival. Also trips on the floating bridge to Torpoint had been regular activities and occasionally I had taken the Cremyll ferry to Mount Edgecombe. In the last few years there had additionally been expeditions which were done once in a blue moon and then never got repeated. They were journeys such as the boat trips to Drake Island, a booze cruise up the Tamar to Calstock, a short voyage across Plymouth Sound to Kingsand and Cawsand and there had been a short ferry jaunt across a river in Cornwall which I think had been the Fowey.

Things like that whole experience in Hungary are without a doubt a matter of personal confidence. The Teach English as a Foreign Language course which I had completed was certainly not a confidence boost however, and I wish it had been. The only part of it which had required any self-belief was the weekend when we students had to spend twenty hours in the company of each other and a tutor. In addition to that it had been a course that took eighty hours of on-line work which I did over about nine months thanks to the local charity organisation Keyham Community Partnership who had allowed me to use their broadband computers for free and those of the local libraries too. I have always been keen to take advantage of anything which equates to a free lunch. I must admit, ever since I was a child I've had a reputation for having empty legs which I used to fill with food at meals. That's why one of my favourite Christmases was the one when Dad and I stayed with my grandparents for a few days and on the day itself we had lunch of a roast chicken with Dad's parents and then took a trip a few miles down the road to Dad's sister whose family always had a roast goose in the evening. Two Christmas dinners in one day: fantastic! The TEFL course had been a Christmas idea too, as around the Christmas of 2007 I had felt my life was going nowhere at a considerable velocity so I had needed to try and find a new target for my efforts and energies. I had decided that a TEFL course would be a good thing to do as it would allow me to get a job in another country. That was a certainty with the company I was looking to use as if I completed the course they provided I was guaranteed a placement in a job in another country.

The reason I had seen that as such as an important factor was my sort of breakdown and the long term result of that, namely that I had a criminal record for the rest of my life. It was like wearing an invisible millstone round my neck when it came to swimming in the job market. Now I can quite understand why people with criminal records need to be checked before working with children and vulnerable individuals but just going by application forms I've filled in I am still wondering why it matters if grave diggers (cemetery maintenance workers) have criminal history.

My dad could see I needed to do something different if I didn't want to continue spending my life just doing voluntary work and being honest on application forms. Therefore when I stayed with him for a few days over Christmas and we talked about the future he was keen on my idea to do the TEFL course and have him pick up the bill as a present. I had certainly felt I would be doing well if I could teach as well as he did, as thanks to him I passed 'A' level Physics, I wouldn't have done it otherwise. Also my aunt had been a respected teacher for years so maybe it was in the family genes.

While doing my degree in Literary Studies with Theology and Philosophy I had taken a couple of chances to do things which may help to increase my self-confidence. Certainly there were parts of the degree course which needed a bit of self-assurance but I also chose a few extra activities which I felt would be beneficial too. By that time I had regularly been standing up in church reading from the Bible and more recently reading prayers which I had written myself. These I wrote on the morning of the service over breakfast while watching the news, so my prayers were always very up to date and I liked to think they made good use of the beautiful English language which I enjoyed so much. I may be wrong but I don't think the other people who wrote prayers did so with a thesaurus in one hand while making a concentrated effort to start each prayer with a different title for God. These were things such as Messiah, Prince of Peace, Christ, Heavenly Father etc.

As our Easy-Jet flight from Gatwick to Budapest cruised over Germany at 27,000 feet, I looked round at the other passengers to see who was accompanying me to the Hungarian capital. I got the impression it was about 50% business and 50% pleasure. I also got the feeling that a small percentage of flyers were not enjoying themselves despite it being so highly rated by statistics in the safety department. I didn't quite know why but seeing a number of people who seemed to be suffering from fear made me recall a literary piece I read years ago by one of my favourite authors. H.P. Lovecraft was considered to be the father of modern Gothic horror and was highly praised by Stephen King, who described him as "The 20th century horror story's dark and baroque prince." However the piece I was thinking of was his essay *Supernatural Horror in Literature* written in 1926-7. The opening passage of that essay stated that fear is the oldest and strongest emotion known to man, particularly fear of the unknown. This generally seemed a sensible concept to me but one thing that was true was that I was going to a country I didn't know to meet some strangers and start doing an unfamiliar job, but I was surprisingly unfearful.

When I sat back and enjoyed the view of what I guessed was central Europe, as we had been flying a while then, I remembered thinking that maybe I just wasn't the kind of person who spent time and energy worrying. This was very unlike a friend of mine who I would write to back home in Plymouth. He was the greatest worrier I had ever known. I recalled an occasion when he had been driving us somewhere and as we got back into the car he paused to look at the tyres. One of them had a stain on and so there was a patch a slightly different colour to the rest of the rubber. It had seemed to me to be about the most insignificant thing imaginable but to him it had been a point of great concern. He had thought that it might indicate a weakness in the tyre and so he feared a blow-out till he had the tyre replaced. He also amused me with his fear of buying electrical goods from charity shops and his aversion to any goods being sold cheap due to best before dates. I found such things an essential part of life as my finances were so restricted I walked round the supermarket looking to see what was on offer or reduced to clear rather than just getting what I felt like having that day. If he compared our existences he would see himself as much closer to normal and maybe even perfection than me. However in response to his thought patterns I had taken my

Moleskine notebook and stuck a sticker on the front which I had bought at the Isle of Wight festival earlier that year. In nice bright orange letters on a glittery purple background it said, "Normal People worry me!" There was only one thing which I was even slightly anxious about at that time. It was that when I met up with the man who was to take me and a guy called Jack from the airport to a hotel they would see the chocolate stain I had on my silk tie. It was the best tie I had brought with me as it was a design unlike any other ties I had ever seen, it had only cost 50p in a charity shop and was made by a company called Rinaldo.

It's a good thing I was there for a unique experience and that I'd a got a good helping of patience in my nature. At Budapest airport I first met up with the man György who worked at Budapest to pick up the TEFL teachers and give them a few days of introduction to Hungary. Then he gave us a few tips and hints on teaching in that country and finally he linked us up with the schools where we were employed. The two of us also met an Australian 26 year old called Jack and went out to catch a taxi. He drove us right through the heart of the city, snatching glimpses of the landmarks, significant buildings and bridges over the River Danube. Eventually we started turning down smaller roads till we pulled up in front of what looked to me to be a dingy hostel. Jack and I were shown upstairs to a flat which had two single beds in the same room, a bathroom, a kitchen and a balcony which looked out over a courtyard at the back. From the balcony I could stand and admire the architecture of suburban Budapest while partaking of a cigarette. As I became more aware of over time, I could smoke just about anywhere in Hungary while back in England it was illegal to smoke in bus stops by then. I've always been the sort of person to go exploring new places and so after a short chat to Jack I set off to investigate this fantastic city which was so steeped in history and was split down the middle by such a marvellous waterway. The Danube was mentioned in one of my all-time favourite Gothic fiction works, as Count Dracula used it for transport.

One of my plans and intentions for all my activities of the upcoming weeks and months was that I would not mislead anybody. To be more specific I was not going to lie and also if I knew something and was in the company of someone else who didn't know it I would tell them of it immediately rather than wait till the subject arose. What I had in mind regarding this at that time was to tell my roommate Jack that if in the early morning he heard me returning to the room and then there was the sound of a disturbance that he didn't need to be distressed as it was probably just me having an epileptic fit as I was only prone to them while entering or exiting consciousness thanks to my current medication.

Looking back on things these days I wish that that night had been the kind of subdued session that had nothing more than a convulsion as its highlight. However I was about to receive an incredible lesson in the trouble a nicotine addiction can get you into. Thanks to having always walked to and from school when I hadn't been a boarder and having boarded at a school where we all had to run for a circuit round the house and garden before breakfast except on Sundays I was quite happy to explore the magnificent surroundings on foot. What struck me as a good idea was to obtain the higher ground so I could take a look about the place and note a few significant landmarks so I made my way up Castle Hill. It was about early dusk time and slowly but surely the light faded over the Houses of Parliament, the assorted Palaces and a very impressive range of Basilica, Cathedrals, churches and chapels. While browsing the stalls and stands at the peak of Castle Hill I decided to buy a shawl type garment, as I expected the country to get considerably colder as the end of the year approached. I also knew it was the kind of thing I could give to a friend of mine back in Plymouth once I returned. At that time I didn't know if that was likely to be at the end of that term or after a whole academic year. Maybe not even then if I met a lovable Hungarian young lady. I had been given such an impression that it would be cold in the winter that I had gone to the trouble of finding myself some thermal undergarments while still back in Plymouth.

Having seen the whole city from a good viewpoint I descended the hill to the nearest bridge and crossed the glorious river to get myself to what appeared to me a walkway similar to the Embankment by the Thames. It gave the impression of being the part of the city which housed the highest quality hotels, restaurants and nightclubs. Unfortunately I had had little time to study Hungary, its language and its capital city as up until a few weeks ago I had thought I was going to be doing my teaching in Greece. Unfortunately I was too late making my application for a place in Greece and they had all been filled due to its popularity. In fact it turned out that there was to be political unrest in Greece, so I wasn't upset to have not made Greece. I had started a CD course of Greek and had spent hours examining books on the phenomenal history of the country, its mythology and I had plans for numerous places to call in on around Athens. Due to missing the Greek placement I was left the choice of Hungary, Honduras and the Czech Republic. I liked the idea of Honduras but imagined it would be too much of a culture shock going to a tropical wilderness having been so contained for most of my life previously. The Czech Republic would have been good but I found they didn't take teachers with criminal records unfortunately. Therefore Hungary was selected. I didn't know how much time I'd have to myself but if possible I'd visit the Transylvanian Alps and spend a night at the Borgo pass to satisfy my sense of Gothic sightseeing. If I found myself at the other end of the country I had plans for another visit with horror connections, but those were real not fictional ones. I can't explain why really but I've always been fascinated by the whole concept of Auschwitz. So I would have taken a trip to the place with the name that is connected to A and Ω, the beginning and the end by having A to start and Z to finish. I think what really intrigues me about the actions of the Holocaust is the way ordinary, everyday Germans were persuaded to be brutal mass murderers so quickly and easily.

However I had been lucky enough to meet a couple via my great aunt who had a relative living in the depths of Hungarian countryside, and so they had told me a few basic words and phrases. I was aware though that it is generally considered to be one of the hardest European languages to master. I wasn't especially looking to take on board too much Hungarian vocabulary as a long term goal I had was to go on and teach English in Moscow or St. Petersburg while learning Russian. Therefore I planned to leave my unallocated memory empty so I could fill it later with Russian words and phrases. I had always enjoyed the classic Russian novels such as *Crime and Punishment, The Brothers Karamazov* and *War and Peace*. Clearly I viewed these things differently to the way many other people did and I often recalled what had happened once at an interview I had for a job I didn't want. The job centre had arranged the meeting between me and the recruitment officer for whichever company it was. I had been doing better than intended throughout our conversation and so I now confess I felt I needed to discourage this man from thinking about employing me. He asked me to tell him something I was proud of, probably hoping I would come up with a week I had achieved better sales figures than anybody else in my team or some other such nonsense. However to deter my potential employer I said I was very proud of having read War and Peace by Tolstoy, and then asked him which of the great Russian novelists he enjoyed. Clearly he didn't have a favourite in that crowd and I got the feeling that reading the weekly TV guide was about the extent of literature in his household.

Chapter 24

As I strolled along the side of the Danube I admired the assorted elegant structures, many of which in this part of town had menus on display in the windows. I was particularly grateful to those who had an English version as well as a Hungarian one. I was surprised to see how much fish was on the menu considering this is a country which didn't have any coastline, though it does have the largest inland body of water in a European country. It would have been at that time that I first added catfish to my list of things to try as it seemed to be on most of the quality food lists. At that time however I was too keen to explore the great city and I only had a limited budget so I decided to leave the catfish for now. Also it was a long time since I had last had a cigarette and despite all efforts I could find no shops where they could be purchased. Then I reached an area where the current walkway opened out into a square in which a brass band was playing what I assumed was traditional Hungarian music. The sky was darkening now but it was still a warm evening and the majority of people seemed to be sitting at tables in the open enjoying food, drink and each other's company.

While I meandered through the dark streets of a historic beautiful city I couldn't help thinking it was the kind of experience which one does enjoy by oneself but it was also the sort of thing that was great to share, be it with other family members, partners or even just acquaintances that aren't really known. Jack was the only person in Budapest who I knew anything about, but what I didn't know was his mobile number so I would have to put up with being isolated. This was not a new or unfamiliar experience as I was an only child and having lost Mum at the age of five, boarding school, then Portland Young Offenders Institution had trained me for independence. Just as I was about to turn and try and find a way back to the hostel I was approached by someone who I could easily have mistaken for a James Bond's villain right-hand man. He was well built under his tuxedo and was clearly familiar with foreigners wandering these notable streets.

"Sir, would you care to enter my reputable establishment for a drink?" he said in slightly sluggish English.

"Maybe a little later, but first I need to find myself a shop to buy some cigarettes." was my reply.

"Come in Sir and I'll find a packet of your chosen brand of cigarettes for you," he responded.

It was at that point the personal safety truism- 'If it seems to be too good to be true it probably is'- should have kicked in. However it was overruled by the axiom I generally used as an excuse after having done something a little reckless, foolish or irresponsible. 'Be spontaneous as one maybe dead this time tomorrow.' (Carpe diem) This had been my common mitigation for when I had indulged in ill-planned financial activity when at Manchester Metropolitan University. I couldn't argue against this as a belief as when Mum was driving me back home after nursery there was the car accident which has never been explained as no other cars were involved and the light, weather etc. were fine. Yet it had led to Mum going from presence in good health to absence due to death within a couple of hours.

So I allowed my Hungarian shopper friend to escort me to his associates standing in a dark doorway which had neon light Hungarian words above it. International pop music and a red glow seeped out from inside with laughter and other alluring things drifting in the surrounding miasma. A step or two in the doorway and I was shown a sharp turn to the right and a curtain was pulled to one side allowing me entry. As I was greeted by a different internal attendant who asked what I wished to drink my previous escort asked me what type of cigarettes I had desired. I asked those eager and enthusiastic servants for a pack of Marlboro Lights, a lighter and a local beer and I took a seat in the nearest booth. I'm not sure precisely what I expected to find in that establishment but I wasn't too surprised to find a stage which was being steeped in dry ice while accommodated a chrome pole, a semi-naked young lady and discarded pieces of elaborate clothing such as thigh length patent leather boots, a feather boa and the type of triangular hat which I associated with historic Naval Officers. While relaxing on the PVC sofa in the booth I observed there were other ones round the wall and many were shut off behind curtains with assorted noises emitting. I was then delivered a well-chilled beer, and an ashtray containing a pack of 20 smokes and a lighter which advertised the establishment on its side. The liquid refreshment was conveyed by a well-built blonde wearing just a bra and panties who came and sat on my right, striking up a conversation on the subject of my knowledge of Budapest. Just as that started I sparked up a smoke and washed it down with cold lager. Then to my astonishment a much smaller darker skinned 'femme fatale' came and sat on my other side.

She whispered in my ear that this place was very well heated and so I should remove my jacket. Not wanting to seem negative or disobliging I confess I quickly did so after ensuring it remained in my vision while all significant possessions were in my trouser pockets. Being jacketless obviously made the undoing of my shirt a much easier venture for the little elfish maiden who I found the more attractive of the two. Whether it is policy at places such as that to give me so much variety with as few girls as possible I didn't know but I thought it worked for sure. I had a pale, strapping great generously breasted Goldilocks carrying shoulder length 'crowning glory' on one side and a featherweight, bob style cut, dark eyes and middle Eastern looking companion on the other. Now the girls and I were getting more familiar which allowed us to do something as a favour for each other. I was soon convinced to buy a round of drinks getting one each for the three of us and in return I had my shirt completely removed and I was smeared and lubricated with baby oil. Such activity was not something I had distinctly asked for but it was a pleasurable way to pass the time in my reckoning. Thus followed what some would call a Karmic principle of "what goes around comes around" I was given an invitation to lubricate each of the girls.

I started by discussing the DJ's choice of music with the one I'll call Midget as she spoke far more fluently while Blondie sat on my thighs facing the same direction as I did. This allowed me to reach in front of me and under her arms to clutch her bountiful bosoms and fondle her nipples greasily. While I debated the pros and cons of current pop music versus the classic artists of the previous era such as Duran Duran, Eurythmics, and Adam and the Ants I enjoyed a quite adequate handful of mammalian glands. I must admit that this was such an alien experience to me I found all sorts of curious thoughts and ideas rushing through my mind. As what I suppose must have been a combination of thinking about my favourite music while having a delightful physical episode I soon had a picture in my mind of Frank Zappa. This hadn't been just any image of the psychedelic rocker, but the one showing him "blackened up" on the cover of *'Joe's Garage'* album; his terrific double disc rock opera. I presumed it was that one as that contains the song Wet T-shirt Contest in which somebody delivers a pun which is the type of humour Mr Zappa and I were entertained by. "Thank you for the mammaries".

Having been taught a considerable number of phrases and expressions in life I was quite aware of 'variety is the spice of life' and so before too long the three of us shuffled about in our curtained compartment. We had a brief interlude in which we sipped our beverages, puffed a couple of ciggies and if I remember right had a brief chat on how each of us had got be where we were and where we planned to go. Then Midget sat on my lap in a side saddle style allowing my right arm to reach round her back to caress one breast while leaning forward permitted sucking the nipple of the other. Meanwhile Blondie massaged my chest with some more lotion and told me how much she liked the feel of my legs and the appearance of my eyes. I could easily explain why I had such well-built muscular legs as I did by telling my new friend of my exercise as a school boy and if back then I had known all the different benefits I would receive from my robust thighs I probably would have volunteered to do extra laps of The Old Ride school grounds. As for my eyes, I'd had a squint surgically corrected years ago but that was more to stop me looking skew-whiff than to improve my sex appeal.

Time progressed and I was an hour off balance already as there we had Central European Time rather than British Summer which I had left behind. Also I got the suspicion I would be requested for another round of drinks soon so I decided it was time to 'escape' at any minute. Having brought a significant wad of Forints with me I requested a bill but was slightly daunted seeing a number with so many zeros on the end of it. However I considered the exchange rate it was reasonable as £10 equated to Ft 2,500. I soon realised I would in fact need some more cash and so I had a chat with the male member of staff in a bow-tie outfit. It didn't take long to realise that this wasn't the first time a foreign visitor to this club had overextended their budget due to unfamiliarity with currency. In fact I had a suspicion it was expected as they had soon found a member of staff free to escort me to the nearest ATM. Thus I was conveyed round a few corners and shown where to place my international credit card.

However I had soon found myself in an even more uncomfortable situation as I had used nearly all the money extracted to clear the slate so I lacked a taxi fare. However remembering procedure at home I thought if I waited till after midnight my credit would be OK again to extract some more Forints.

Chapter 25

Now I needed to find a way to pass a few hours in an unknown city where I spoke a language that few of the population seemed to know a word of. I can't recall quite where it came from but I got myself a part empty can of lager. I assumed I had gained this by what in Plymouth we called 'minesweeping.' I expect it was while doing that I met two girls who were German tourists and they could speak quite reasonable English. However there was some misunderstanding between us which didn't become clear till later. They invited me to join them for a bite to eat in their hotel so I eagerly consented to that proposition. It was probably about that time I lost my bearing as we walked from the area of quality hostelries and guesthouses. We entered the taverna style restaurant in the basement of their hotel and quickly settled at a table which allowed us a good view of the evening's entertainment.

On a slightly raised stage was a keyboard player providing backing for a singer who had performed classic smoochy songs for a few pairs on the dance floor. If I had seen such an artist at home I would have thought 'mutton dressed as lamb' but mutton was so highly rated here that that didn't really work. As our food arrived she took a break and the keyboard player set his equipment to release a melody or two on auto-pilot. As Lady Lamb strolled over to the bar, one of my German friends asked her if she would do any requests. She joined us at our table and over a few glasses of wine and a Greek style meal it was concluded that once our meal had gone down she would sing a few ABBA songs and so encourage slightly more vigorous dancing. I was quite satisfied with this as an ABBA LP had been part of the limited music collection around me through my teenage years. My companions gave the impression they often did this, but I wasn't a frequent dancer and when I had moved to music it had been more likely to be Guns n' Roses, Metallica or Motorhead. We all seemed to enjoy ourselves and we even got some others to join us. I chose to sit out 'Money, Money, Money,' as it didn't seem to suit me at that time, but while doing so I was delivered the bill. I explained I needed to visit a cash machine and so left to do so. Unfortunately I had been mistaken in my supposition regarding midnight and my finances and so I failed to return, which was a shame as I had enjoyed the Anglo-German relationship we had established.

Then I found myself lost in an alien city with no money, no ability to communicate and nobody I knew within thousands of miles. If that had been described to me previously I think I would have predicted I would have been quite distressed but I was seriously surprised by how unworried I was. It then got much colder as the sky was clear and so no heat was being retained. Also, as I had not planned to be out for any serious length of time, I wasn't wearing my full length SS officer's coat. When I had been in England and found myself in exceedingly difficult situations my last resort response was to phone home using a reverse charge phone call if necessary. Considering that Dad was thousands of miles away that didn't seem to be a worthwhile activity at that time. My phone had just about run out of charge as well, to add insult to injury. Recalling a park I had walked through near the Castle Hill earlier I remembered there had been people out on the streets looking like Budapest's equivalent to homeless street alcoholics. That appeared to me to be a good thing as it meant the police obviously didn't come down too hard on such individuals if they kept out of the way and didn't cause trouble, so if I could find a quiet, warm covered car park or doorway I could curl up for a few hours to gain some sleep. Personally I had no experience of being homeless and sleeping rough but it didn't scare me too much as back in Plymouth one of my best friends had done so for weeks in the bleak mid-winter and been in his 60's at the time. That character had my extensive gratitude as, while I was in Hungary, he was looking after Alice, the one-eyed wonder cat.

As a distraction from the cold climate I was enduring I recalled the incredible way my friend and I had initiated our friendship. A cold, wet December evening years ago, I had walked from my flat to the local shopping area with banknotes in my pockets and no change. I came round the corner and was hailed by a chap who looked so gaunt he made an anorexic skeleton seem obese.

"Hey, buddy can you lend us a dime?" was his greeting.

Usually if asked for money by an apparently destitute soul I'd ignored them or said I had enough problems of my own, like telling a Big Issue seller I had my own sizable issues.

But for some inexplicable reason that time I had replied, "I've got no change at the minute, but wait here and I'll give you a £1 coin when I get back!"

That was accepted and so after picking up that day's supply of white cider in blue plastic bottles I had returned and gave my "buddy" a £1 coin. He said he had meant it when he just said lend it and so he asked my address so he could pay me back tomorrow. I confess I hadn't believed it but felt it could do no harm and so told him of my flat on Queens Road. When Steve John Dixon Wilson had rung my doorbell the following morning just after 9 o'clock with a pound coin I realised that retired RAF Cornishmen didn't say something without meaning it or, '20,000 Cornishmen will know the reason why.' Thus began a friendship with 'Dogend' Wilson which lasted for 20 years or so.

Chapter 26

Sun 14/09/2008. I had continued wandering round the Budapest Utcas (Hungarian streets), keeping moving to retain a level of heat within my body. As it was now past midnight and thus Sunday the churches had started to rise for the weekly peak of their activity. I came across one which had tables in the courtyard loaded with consumables and it seemed they were priming for a wedding reception. Unfortunately they had seemed paranoid that passers-by would try and help themselves and I couldn't find any English speakers as I had hoped to request a little Christian charity from a Good Samaritan. I was quite happy not to try the victuals; I just wanted a little direction and would have been incredibly thankful for a taxi fare.

By then I had been peregrinating for so long my feet hurt and I sought a rest. I had felt it was probably a good thing I had experienced pedal discomfort to a great degree a couple of years ago at the Isle of Wight festival, having worn the wrong shoes and so being in such pain at one stage I had to crawl or slide along on my posterior for a while till my senses had been dulled by alcohol or narcotics (not necessarily illegal products). Eventually I had a stroke of luck as I came across an Internet cafe. However it was about 9 o'clock and the cleaner there hadn't known if 10 or 11 was the opening time on a Sunday. Still I had hope and having read in the window that 150 Forints (Ft) would get me a session and I had a 200 Ft note I just needed to wait. I borrowed a bench for a catnap and asked the cleaner to tell the workers there to wake me just after 11. I must admit I think I was rather clever with my sort of detective work I did then to find the address I needed.

Calling up my Yahoo e-mail I had found what I had been send by György as he had said he meant to meet me at the airport but if for some reason that failed I had also been supplied with the address of our hostel. So I therefore had the address I was seeking and I asked the cafe worker for the address of the establishment. Now I had A and B and during the night to pass time I had popped in to the reception of a distinguished looking hotel and found it stored numerous pamphlets and brochures of the principal tourist attractions. Many of those contained maps showing where in the city they were and I had picked up the best one so I had a free Budapest Utcas map. Ironically I found I was 5 minutes' walk from my target and had been walking within a short distance of it for a lot of the night. Once I got back I found the room was empty as Jack had obviously gone in search of a Hungary breakfast and to take part in a more successful exploration of the city. I simply crashed out and left my phone to charge, having been sensible enough to bring a travel adapter with me.

When I woke up I found that, due to the type of lock system employed I was locked in till Jack returned. When he returned he gave me György's phone number but for some reason it didn't connect so Jack sent him a text to say I was still alive and OK. Following that, Jack introduced me to the other TEFL teachers in the party. There was Beth, a 22 year old Hong Kong Chinese woman who had lived in Australia but was using TEFL as a way to travel the world. Liz was an attractive 20 year old American exploring Europe and teaching now and then to maintain her bank account. The one I got on with best was Pam from London. She was a 55 year old Londoner who had used TEFL as a fresh start after a mid-life crisis.

For some reason nobody had successfully get any hot water previously but now could and so we engaged in a brief coffee session. Someone had brought some Douwe Egberts filter coffee with them from their last residence but had no filter. I don't know if he thought of it then or he'd done it before but Jack suggested we make the coffee and then allow gravity to subdue the granules so we had a quality caffeine supply with the grains being in relation to how hot you had wanted your hit. If you didn't mind cold coffee you could have had it grainless.

I had decided if I told people what had happened the night before I would look very foolish and might get in trouble with somebody. So as a cover story I said I had been pick-pocketed while on Castle Hill and had lost my wallet and my map. Hence I had been lost all night but had been salvaged by the local constabulary. It had soon became clear these guys knew the Good Samaritan principle as following our coffee session it was decided to have a Chinese meal in a large restaurant in a few hours. I had expected to go to a local establishment but it made sense thinking we had been about to start a period in which we would be eating very little except Hungarian cuisine. Also our colleague Beth had felt it was time to practice her Mandarin speaking skills which seemed quite reasonable. Fortunately for me Jack was a nicotine addict too so he kindly gave me enough Forints to buy myself a packet of cigarettes.

We then returned to our dreary rooms, the ladies in one and Jack and I next door. I had hoped to get to know my roommate a little better but I was so tired after the night before I fell asleep pretty much as soon as I touched the bed. Meanwhile Jack watched a film on his laptop. Once or twice during the night I woke up. Firstly needing a little relief and I think secondly having had a *grand mal* seizure but as it involved loss of consciousness it was hard to be sure as it occurred while I was asleep. However looking at the tangled state my blankets and sheets were in I think it was a fairly safe bet. Still, I just needed to get through one more night and then I'd be moved to my own place. That was because one of the terms and conditions of my contract was that the school provided me with my own flat and meals on weekdays.

Mon 15/09/2008

Next morning I had a rummage through my suitcase and found some Penguin chocolate biscuits which made a quite reasonable breakfast as I was looking to spend as little money as possible for the time being. The rest of the party went down and had a meal of fresh fruit from a local corner shop. Then we walked to the neighbourhood Metro station to meet György. I must admit all in all I was quite impressed by his manner. I told him my cover story about having been pick-pocketed and he certainly seemed to believe me as he didn't wait long to tell me I smelt like a homeless person so I gave him 10/10 for honesty. He then paid for my Metro ticket and we went to a school on the edge of the city centre which we were told was the equivalent of a USA High school or British Comprehensive. However it was one that would have been quite high up the league tables.

I hadn't been told but the others had been told to prepare lessons plans for that day and so they took turns in delivering their first lessons to Hungarian students. I think the essential discovery at this point was that the students were much better than we had all expected. Particularly as English was an extra language after German for many of them. We were all pleased about that and concluded we could do a lot better when we had syllabuses and so had clear-cut guidelines of what precisely to focus on.

After the teaching practice we took a ride back to the square we had caught the Metro from that morning as it had an adjacent shopping centre. I had been given 2,500 Ft by György and also a generous parcel of personal hygiene products by then. By good fortune I stayed with Pam for my first sample of Hungarian fast food and following it I was shown a historic looking building on the corner of the square which contained a language school on the third floor. György hadn't shown me that was the place we were supposed to meet up at for 2 o'clock. That gave me 20 minutes for my first good look at one of Budapest's equivalents to Drake Circus or the Arndale, which are the two shopping centres I know best. That was where and when I started to understand why Hungary doesn't have the obesity problem that prevails in the UK. The shopping centres in Britain rarely have any greengrocers and if so it would be an isolated backwoods trader struggling against the supermarkets. I was amazed to find that there are more food emporiums than anything else, and the majority had stalls out front loaded with fresh fruit and vegetables. They provided everything I was familiar with and also goods like little celariacs and giant horseradishes. There was an abundance of yellow capsicum which I dare say was expected as my dad had passed rapidly through Hungary in the past and had said he saw bountiful supplies of peppers everywhere like it was the national fruit. He had passed through on his way to and from Romania in 1991 driving a truck to an orphanage with two very good friends. One was a social worker and the other the local vicar and that was one of a number of community based projects they engaged in. I would have like to join them but unfortunately I was being detained at Her Majesty's Pleasure at the time. The shopping centre had one store of great personal interest as I recognised a second-hand clothing shop selling the kind of things charity shops supplied in Britain, but there it was done for private profit.

I reached the ground floor door of the language school and had a cigarette while I waited. Ten minutes past two had arrived but my companions had not. Luckily when Pam had shown me the building during lunch break she had also rung the intercom to confirm which floor we were looking to meet on. Therefore I knew which button to press to ask about any sign of activity. It was soon revealed that everyone else was already in situ and had begun the afternoon session. I must admit that had made me feel somewhat disappointed in György and Pam, as I thought they should have either told me to go straight into position or waited for me at the downstairs entrance. Concluding directness appealed to György from the way he had spoken to me previously I entered the room and sat down saying, "You don't make it very easy to find you guys!"

I found I had missed the beginning of a teaching methodology video and PowerPoint presentation. It seemed to be tips for educators universally rather than specific Hungarian based guidelines. It particularly had games we could use to fill in the last few minutes of a lesson in a productive way. It was a short piece and so we soon had an interval in which we could use the language school's internet connected computers and, if I remember rightly, this was where I first encountered the Hungarian keyboard. It has two significant differences to the standard QWERTY board which I knew and loved. The primary alteration was that it was QWERTZ as the Y and Z are swapped and also as many Hungarian vowels can be encountered with various accents over them. The alternative vowels filled the keys on the right hand side. Slightly slowed by seeking my e-mail on Zahoo till I noticed the mistake, I used the opportunity to de-Spam my inbox. Then I contacted my dad saying everything was "peachy, creamy" and omitting any mention of my tight finances as I felt it was my problem being my fault.

We then reassembled in the classroom and were invited to ask any questions. The other four all asked about the schools they were being sent to. I had already ascertained a fair knowledge of mine, Bonyhádi Petőfi Sándor Evangélikus Gimnázium, as György had sent me their website. One thing which had impressed me about it was that it was written in Hungarian but by clicking an icon of a national flag it could be translated to English or German. Another thing I liked about it was that it had been done by the students and gave an all-embracing picture of the college; past and present. Additionally it talked about equipment and facilities as well as customs and traditions. I got the impression the other schools didn't have websites as nobody else seemed to know a thing about their places beyond where in Hungary they were situated. The two 'girlies' were both staying in Budapest while Jack went north towards the mountains and could easily have made a trip to Transylvania which I would have done. Pam was being dispatched to a place on the shore of Lake Balaton and I was going across the Great Hungarian Plain to a small town called Bonyhád. It turned out I was the only one teaching at a boarding school, which suited me fine as I could relate to children separated from parents following my upbringing which started boarding at about seven years old.

We then returned to the hotel briefly and I used the interlude to phone the credit card company. I soon found that it wasn't 'the end of the world' as I still had £500 (Ft 125,000) credit. I don't know when it started but for years then every time I was in a difficult situation or something had gone seriously wrong I would console myself by saying "it's not the end of the world" which I found a very comforting and effective morale booster. We then went to one of the many Hungarian cuisine eating houses in the area and found a menu with an English translation. I could have been more explorative in my choice but thought I knew what I was doing with 'noodles with cottage cheese and bacon crackling'. Everything on the menu seemed to be ingredients I knew in combinations I didn't with a few exceptions such as catfish. However I was surprised when a platter of what appeared to be lasagne broken into strips wider than tagliatelle in a cottage cheese sauce arrived topped with a lake of sour cream and bacon rind clippings. Between the five of us (as György had returned home by now) we used a pitcher of local lager to dispatch our meals and then I departed for a walk in the rain.

I was glad that it had been the previous night I had been out on the streets as that night it was pouring felines and canines. I wondered what it would be like trying to explain to my enthusiastic students how and why we English talked about animals coming out of the sky in inclement weather. Still I was keen to learn about their verbal idiosyncrasies too. I was OK that night as when my full length SS garment was secured with a good pair of boots it kept out all moisture. I strolled to the end of the road containing our hostel and encountered a Roman Catholic Church complex. I was a Protestant myself, but I greatly favoured an ecumenical, multi-faith viewpoint having studied Christians, Buddhists, Muslims, Atheists and Romantics in my degree. In the church hall something was clearly happening at 8 o'clock but, not understanding a word, I didn't know what. Admittedly I suspected it was an AA meeting or similar as through the wide open double doors I saw people sitting in a circle and a lot looked like they had been on the streets in the rain for considerable time. Quite possibly it was weeks since some had washed or shaved by appearances. The fact I had read in a Rough Guide to Hungary a few days before that the country had the highest suicide rate in Europe was brought to mind. Apparently their obituary would say "he/she suddenly tragically left," as a euphemism.

Truly, I believed I had a bit of a reputation for being curious and explorative as a youth and so would always "go and have a look" rather than just sit and wait. I would "give it a go" rather than watch someone else doing it. I had been given detention and a few canings for this but looking back on it now I'm glad, though maybe not then. These days it seems to me people are too wrapped in cotton wool and are certainly doing that to their children. I had hoped to hear a few tales of expeditions in the Outback from Jack as I could tell him a few Dartmoor tales. However a trip to the local supermarket in Sydney had seemed to try his bravery unless done in a taxi aided by his big brother or father. Therefore when he raised the subject of going "for a drink" I encouraged him with wholehearted gusto. As it happened he had seen a place up the road called "John Bull Public House," and they had advertised Guinness in the window. Together we got the two young girls to join what Jack considered our life-threatening journey, but we were doomed as that night there was a private party and Jack wasn't interested if his goal of Guinness could not be reached. It wasn't for me to debate the issue with my fellow TEFLers at that time, but I couldn't understand people sitting in a dingy little room watching a movie (seen before so they had memorised the script) on a laptop in preference to exploring the historic walks of a fabulous metropolis such as those of the twin cities Buda and Pest united across the Danube. It is a place that has seen Empires rise and fall, revolutions go round, and occupiers come and go so I preferred it to the latest episode of the Halloween films. Admittedly I might have got a bit wet but that seemed a reasonable sacrifice for memories I would treasure for the rest of my life.

As I had expected, homesickness wasn't a problem for me, though this was a bit early in the trip to really judge having only been away for a couple of days so far. However I had been at boarding school on and off between seven and eighteen, following that with eighteen months in prison so I hadn't seen it as a threat. Also I thought that, having lost my mum at the age of five and various friends dying or committing suicide between then and leaving the prison gates, I was probably quite capable of being emotionally resilient. I had numerous recollections of events such as at Prep school when I was glad to be back in school at the start of term and I thought the boys who were older than me but were in tears the first night had a lot of growing up still to do. Also there had been one time at my main school when in the middle of a biology lesson a senior teacher had interrupted our study of osmosis to say that the reason our classmate Julian Wakeham wasn't in that day was that he had been found dead in his bedroom that morning. This, in theory, should have hit me harder than the other members of class 5B as I had been round to his house and met his Blue Persian cat a few times. Even more significant was that the previous summer he had come with my dad and me on a sailing holiday round the Norfolk Broads. The rest of the class didn't burst into a deluge of tears but the girls started to whimper and the guys were seriously subdued for the rest of the double period. I was so phlegmatic by then that I wanted to get back to the semi-permeable membranes and Brownian motion.

I confess I had been additionally keen to leave behind in England acquaintances that had regularly sent me streams of texts asking if I would come and do them various favours. These ranged from one girl I had known for years and supported to the best of my abilities as my Christian morality told me to do so. She would regularly ask me if she could come to my place to get drunk and so temporarily forget her latest domestically violent partner. On the other end of the scale was a factory worker who had an abhorrent shift starting in the middle of the afternoon and concluding just before midnight. I hardly ever saw him during the week but I could be pretty sure of an invitation to his flat at the weekend for a generous supply of intoxicants. Quite possibly these people were missing me, but at the time I had been too engrossed in new experiences to give their absence any consideration. In fact, due to my sense of humour and emotional indifference, I had been very tempted to take the postcards I had brought with me which bore messages such as "Wish you were here" and "Call me!" and turn them negative by applying a 'don't' to the start and send them to specific people. However I wasn't really that cold-blooded and so I decided against it.

Jack seemed OK keeping himself to himself while I lay on my bed and wrote my diary listening to assorted music which I had recorded on a 2G memory card in the days before departure. The pieces I was listening to in that environment ranged from wonderfully harmonious compositions by Arvo Pärt (Estonian), to Pink Floyd instrumental albums. A. Pärt, my favourite modern composer was very keen on 'tintinnabuli' and 'minimalist' writing, and so provided marvels such as *'Spiegel im Spiegel.'* That was suitable at that time as I found if I listened to music with words while writing or reading I got distracted. It was usually alright if the words were in a foreign language as my inability to comprehend them prevented them being side-tracking. After updating the diary I returned to reading *'Morality Play'* by Barry Unsworth which I had picked up in the Torpoint St. Luke's Hospice charity shop because I liked the title, the money (ten pence) went to a good cause and it had been shortlisted for a literature award.

I had been wearing my combat trousers which had the camouflage pattern on except in the colours red, black and white so I told people they were for hiding above the snow line on the top of an active volcano. Anyway it seemed György didn't like them as he said not to wear them next day, yet I didn't need to wear a suit and tie. I'd probably put on a suit without a tie as I hadn't got that many other clothing options. Alternatively I could have used my blue suit jacket as a blazer with a pair of smart jeans which should be enough. One thing I'd been very aware of when we were at the Budapest comprehensive school earlier that day was that my colleagues wore jeans and sweatshirt type items as did the pupils so I couldn't tell them apart which I didn't think was a good thing. I'd yet to see if this was a one off or if Hungarian schools were generally non-uniformed.

I was very glad I'd got a quality Nokia phone that had connecting me to the World Wide Web included in its contract. Already I'd found that was a beneficial facility and by the end of the trip I surmised it to be life, or at least sanity, saving. To pass a little time before we went to bed I cleared out the radio stations I had in the memory from back in Plymouth and used the FM search function to see what I could locate. It revealed BBC World Service and 18 other stations, a few of which were English speaking and the majority were Hungarian with music from classical, to modern pop and local folk. I hoped some of those were all across the country not just in Budapest as the town Bonyhád was deep in the boondocks.

Chapter 27

Tues 16/09/2008. For the first time in ages I'd woken up having slept right through from when I closed my eyes to the time to rise and shine, time for 'hands off cocks, hands on socks' as they used to say when I was in army camps round Great Britain as part of my Combined Cadet Force training. Every night before that for a noticeable period I had woken up at least once in the middle of the night with no explainable cause and usually had a cigarette then (sometimes containing *Cannabis sativa* or *C. indica*).

I went out to Hungary to be a teacher, but that morning I received a lesson. It was in the subject of supply and demand but also related to transportation. I had been very pleased a few weeks ago to find a sizable suitcase going for the bargain price of £5 in a PDSA charity shop. I had been packing my combat trousers, books, shoes, suits and ties in the case when, while trying to do it up, the tags on the zips came off in my hand making securing it sealed a real issue. However I managed to substitute the tags with a length of wire I looped through the space which a padlock fitted through if being used. Just as I proceeded to wheel the case downstairs thinking how well I had improvised a solution, the wheels on the bottom of the case and the case itself parted company. Thus I was left with about an hour to transport my suitcase across the square, past the Roman Catholic Church at the end and over a number of Metro lines, as it seemed to be a place where separate lines met each other at a kind of interchange.

As I was dedicated to travelling lightly I took as little in my suitcase as I could and I had a Ralph Lauren leather holdall for my hand luggage which was being used as a portable library and so was ridiculously heavy in relation to its size. That was a well-planned technique as the defining fact for the suitcase was its weight but hand luggage was defined by size as it had to be able to fit under the seat. I must confess I had been looking to embellish my belongings along the way of my journey and so the hostel provided a couple of personal hygiene products and of rather more value, a towel. As people who are versed in the compositions of Douglas Adams will be aware, a towel is considered an indispensable item for those hitch-hiking the galaxy so I felt greatly heartened once I had one in my possession.

After a backbreaking exertion which I can imagine being part of the basic Marine commando training, in which I moved my two bags to the language school where we were going to be united with someone from our school, I was glad we were expecting Hungarian nibbles and refreshment. I had no idea what to anticipate for Hungarian nibbles but was eager to find out as there are pleasingly few foodstuffs I don't enjoy. Undeniably I do agree with Dr Johnson regarding a particular fodder though. "A cucumber should be well sliced, and dressed with pepper and vinegar, and then thrown out, as good for nothing." Clearly the man was a genius. I also had great expectations for a few restaurant dishes such as catfish or giblet stew.

This trip to Europe to teach received notable support and encouragement from my fellow church members back in Stoke Damerel, one of the oldest churches in Plymouth, and really close to my heart as my dad had been baptised there a while ago. I had been given a number of cards, pictures and indeed Forints and tips by the congregation but it wasn't till then that I understood what someone said about maintaining my Englishness. All the other members of the TEFL party were clad in jeans and tee-shirts while I was decked out in full pin-stripe suit and tie. I think this was probably due to a collection of factors. My attendance of two quite traditional boarding schools primarily, and just having come from a family steeped in naval upbringing being a strong contributory factor. I remember I had the routine of underpants then shirt over them, then trousers secured by belt over them to hold them in place being drilled into my subconsciousness every morning for years at The Old Ride preparatory school.

It was about that time I started finding out what sense of humour my new employers had regarding words and spelling. That being that I could introduce myself as follows. "Hello! My name is Bridgwater, James Bridgwater. That's without an 'e'" and see if they then write Bridgwater in the mountain of paperwork. This was always a serious point of concern with my dad and I, as most people, even some close friends regularly displeased us by using the spelling selected in the northern part of England used for identifying canals in the Mancunian area. The Somerset town famous for its carnival and neighbouring bay lacked a second 'e'. I joined everyone at the language school in reasonable time and soon encountered what turned out to be the first of a number of high points that day. I was greeted by Pam who said I looked smart and so I felt it had been worthwhile going to the trouble of bring suits properly packed into a suitcase rather than just rolled up in a rucksack. It was rewarding that I was the one person there really done up to the nines and the one representing England. After all, I had gone to the trouble of packing a clothes brush as I knew Alice had shed a considerable quantity of fur on the majority of my vestments, and so that had come with me.

I then discovered that Hungarian finger food consisted of a wide range of salamis and cheeses on assorted breads with olives, pieces of pickled peppers accompanied by dips of sour cream and such. The school's representatives turned up in good time, but I was daunted for at least a few minutes as they continued to speak Hungarian to each other for a while. Once we made it to their car Alfréd and Jolán broke into English and things started to pick up. I was told they were a married couple who both worked in the Gimnázium, but unfortunately not in the English department which was a shame as they were both easy going and I reckoned in their late twenties or early thirties. That seemed fine for their plans as she was pregnant and expecting delivery in mid-December. He was involved in the physical education department and also gave karate lessons as an extra-curricular activity to any of the local students, as it turned out there was another secondary school in the little town of just over 14,000 souls. I arranged at that point to find him in a few weeks to get some karate tuition myself but that never worked out. It would have been easy to follow up if I really wanted, as I discovered they had a flat on the floor below me when mine was allocated. This was organised so if I had any problems while getting established I could go down and knock on the door of people who spoke quite respectable English and who knew what I was on about.

We then spent the next few hours driving across the Great Hungarian Plain which looked similar to the way I imagined states like Kansas to be. An immensely open sky over an equally extensive arable spread. I had looked forward to seeing a Brobdingnagian expanse of sunflowers but it emerged I was a few weeks too late for that and so we passed endless acreage of tall dead plants. We passed a couple of impressive sights in both the natural and artificial departments. While driving through a village we came across a wooden electricity/phone line pylon which had a stork nest balanced on top. It was the kind of sight my grandparents would have enjoyed, having both been keen ornithologists. Then for my dad's delight we viewed what I was told was Hungary's sole power station and for particular appreciation with it being a nuclear establishment. This would have gratified him as he pays considerable attention to ideas such as world climate change, drainage of fossil fuels, recyclable energy and particularly world over-population.

We drove into Bonyhád from the east, as that was the side which had a motorway type road passing it by. That meant we passed nearly all significant town features on the way to the school. Just after leaving the motorway we passed the Tesco complex containing a sizable Tesco hypermarket, a coffee shop, pharmacy, bookshop, tobacconist, phone shop, and a couple of clothes boutiques. Then we passed through the heart of the town, driving round the square which was lined with shops and contained the Roman Catholic Church in its centre. This was also the location of the town museum and a couple of drinking establishments. Exiting the square heading west, we had a short drive of about half a mile to the Gimnázium.

I had a rough idea what to expect as their website had a clever photo taken from the heart of the school grounds and rotating to show the surroundings as seen from the middle. Also I had used Google Earth to take a bird's eye view of the town to get an idea of the geography to expect. However none of those enlightened me enough to expect the glorious 1870's building which greeted me. It was the kind of structure that I could have imagined being the home of a psychotic doctor or scientist in a 1970's Hammer horror film. It had a magnificent main entrance accessed by a short path between fir trees to a number of stairs up to the antique doorway. The door had probably been in place since construction not far from 150 years ago. A solid, dark, heavy wooden door with iron hinges and riveted bands, adorned with an exceedingly sturdy lion's head knocker in the centre. Behind that was a porch, more stairs up to the ground floor and a set of double doors to the corridor which was at the heart of the structure. The porch was walled with unshakable stone blocks and it was large enough to house an exhibition.

At that time it was decked with high quality colour photos of items from the surrounding natural world such as close-ups of flowers, fungi and insects, so it seemed to be focused on intimate details. At times while I worked there that changed to hand drawn pictures of medieval life and relating structures such as castles and also the residences of the not so wealthy peasants. That and many later activities encouraged me to think Hungarians were very proud of their history and with good reason.

I was lead across the corridor to the staff room and shown to what would be my centre of educational operations in the English supplies and assets corner. Those walls were lined with shelves heavily stacked behind glass doors from the floor up to ceiling ten feet above the parquet flooring.

Bonyhád struck me as a town about the same size as Tavistock and this was a fairly accurate guess as I later found Bonyhád to have a population of about 14,000 and Tavistock had about 12,000. It was very ironic that Tavistock came to my mind on my arrival in the town, as I soon found out. In the staff room I was introduced to most of the other English teachers there and also a few others including the gentleman with the desk next to mine. In physical appearance he can best be described as someone who could ideally have played Santa Claus, as he was rotund with whitening hair and a very jolly nature polished with an infectious smile. I soon discovered he had been a music teacher who had been at the school for years but now due to his increased years only worked part-time. While talking to the English teachers it soon became clear to them that I had come from Plymouth and this was the point at which I had my first really earth shaking surprise, as a small, energetic woman told me she had been to Plymouth, Tavistock and Barnstable previously to that year with a group of students and they were planning to do it again. The next time however they planned to include a trip to the Big City, possibly calling in at Oxford on the way. Via the Internet they had booked a few rooms in a place at Barnstable and used that as their headquarters from which to explore Devon. As I found out later, a slow rural lifestyle was very characteristic of this part of Hungary, and so there were similarity between them and the Devonians.

This school certainly reminded me of my prep school, The Old Ride, and when I had to go to the Headmaster's office it was done out with dark wooden panels on the wall just like I had known before. I did feel very nervous standing in front of the Head's desk and I think I expected him to reach behind a bookcase, get out a cane and tell me to adopt the position. However he quickly asked me to go through to the next room and we had an interesting conversation as he spoke no English, I spoke no Hungarian and so the lively little lady acted as a translator between the two of us. She became one of my best friends by the time I left.

Lunch, the Hungarian meal of the day was a fantastic spicy noodle soup followed by a fresh peach. It turned out that I would have soup of some sort every day I had lunch in the school, yet the size of some of the pieces of chicken and vegetables floating in some soups made them hard to distinguish from stews or casseroles.

Then I was driven the equivalent of a five minute walk to my flat, which was more than satisfactory. It was on the top floor in an estate of about five identical blocks and one larger block with a greater number of floors and more flats on each floor. It was revealed to me that four floors was very common for Hungarian architecture, as above that they were required to have a lift. The estate wasn't bleak in the least but did remind of estates I had seen in documentaries about conditions in countries behind the Iron Curtain. The flat itself was noticeably larger than mine at home yet had the same rooms, i.e. two bedrooms, one for use as an office, a kitchen, a bathroom and a living room. The living room had a door which led to a balcony from which I could see the sunset.

A potential timetable had been presented to me which gave me three day weekends if I accepted it, but I was sure Jolán (Jola) hadn't been joking when she said they could always find work for me to do if I wanted to come in at any other times. The timetable was a schedule I could relate to from previous experience, being the same distribution of lessons and intervals with a lunch break as I had known at school. The principal difference was that I had had my first lesson starting at 9:00 but in Hungary it was at 7:45! I asked Alfred where the nearest shop was and took a quick trip in the dark unknown to buy unfamiliar foodstuffs in a totally uncharted landscape, so as to have something to finish the day with and some caffeine and sucrose input in the next morning. To finish the day I sifted through the TV channels and found two English speakers out of about 15-20 options. I was planning to use my time in Hungary for reading and writing and that looked as if it would encourage that as it offered limited distraction. I had only CNN and BBC Prime which seemed to cover Europe.

Chapter 28

Wed 17/09/2008. What a day! Once I had sat down on the comfortable sofa in my living room and loaded up with high density coffee and a banana I had felt ready to take on the world, despite the fact the sun wasn't fully up yet and it was shockingly early in the day. I hadn't bought any cigarettes the night before, and so passed a tobacco-free night for the first time in ages. I planned to use Hungary as an aid to giving up and it seemed viable then. Done out in a smart grey suit with a quality shirt and tie, I saw I was the central focus point of the locals as I walked to work and even more so once on the school grounds. I couldn't be sure, as I wasn't fluent in the Finno-Ugric lingo of Magyar, but I got the impression some children were laughing at me but I've always enjoyed making people laugh so I didn't find that a problem.

The sensation of suddenly finding I was walking down the corridor to face my first class of teenage Hungarians reminded me of my first serious sexual experience, as they were both things I had anticipated for a considerable time and had been keen to engage in. However it was also an event I had hoped to do well in, giving the other party a quality, memorable experience but I was very doubtful. It was a fascinating encounter abruptly being on the 'wrong' side of the desk. It quickly developed into what felt like me playing "Just a minute!" The topics being myself, my history, my home, my life, my family and basically my anything. I'm sure the scrappy little picture I had of Alice squatting under a bureau peering out with her singular eye won me lots of points, particularly with the girls. Soon I altered the rules of the game and started to get the students involved. That was a small class of about ten students who were some of the school's best English scholars. What I found most interesting was getting them to tell me about their plans for the future and what they hoped to do or to be after school days. The shocking thing was hardly any of them had any ideas, and it was as though they hadn't even contemplated it. However a couple mentioned a subject which a phenomenally large number of people seemed enthusiastic about. Architecture! When I repeated this style of introduction over the next couple of weeks, as some classes I only had fortnightly, the size of the company wanting to be architects was unnatural. Another thing which became clear in these early sessions was that it was fine to plan to be an architect or to follow in the parents business or trade, yet designs didn't necessarily work out as when I was their age I didn't picture myself in Hungary teaching English with the various life experiences I had now compiled. Admittedly, like a lot of them I didn't really have many other ideas either. By the time I was eighteen I had realised I wouldn't get my dream job of being the Next Generation David Attenborough and so had to think again.

The second class of the morning was more the kind of students I could relate to as they were in a group of about twenty five and it was quickly made clear that certain members took advantage of this by sitting in the back rows and quietly chatting with each other. This was very reflective of me and my school behaviour, not bad but not goody-two-shoes either. The criminals who committed the misdemeanours rather than the felonies. Probably they had the ability to succeed should they want to, but putting in the effort was the hard part. Even those days I was still the sort of worker who could procrastinate for a profession; when it came to reports, essays or dissertations it was always a case of an intense rush at the end rather than a sensible spread out schedule. Those lessons I shared with Terézia (Teréz), who seemed to be the member of staff designated to be my 'buddy'. She appeared to be surprisingly impressed with how the first couple of lessons had gone and so was I.

In the break after that, at the time of day I was used to have my breakfast but was now was having elevenses, I went for a second talk with "The Big Man" in which we discussed a few practicalities such as salary and a few details of things required for the flat. It was at that point I was asked to give the keys up for an hour to the 'Handyman' who worked on the school grounds and also attended the flats which the college either owned or rented. Quite what he did to it then I don't know as it seemed untouched when I returned to it. At that time I was aware of being in a post-Soviet country which, for some reason may have related to the Handyman's appearance. I could easily have imagined him having been in with the KGB and I confess I feared he went and installed a 'bug' in my flat so I could be monitored. Sometimes over the months of our relationship he seemed to understand me with no trouble, but then I asked what he had needed my keys for and I seemed to be unintelligible. Once the keys were back in my possession I had lunch of a curious soup with even stranger, spherical type Unidentified Floating Objects in it - Hungarian croutons, I discovered. That was then followed by deep fried fish pieces with potato salad, but I was too preoccupied to inquire as to whether it was catfish, as it seemed that was a restaurant fish. One doesn't get sea bass or salmon at school so I guessed it was equivalent to the same there.

Then I decided to brave the 'Superunknown' as one of my favourite bands would probably have described it and so I set off in to the heart of Bonyhád or Bonehead as it often came up in search engines. It was certainly much to my advantage that Lidl's and Aldi's are trans-European stores and ones I was very familiar with from back home. I found them to be the cheapest providers of most personal hygiene products, but hadn't stuck with one specifically. Therefore I packed Lidl razorblades with an Aldi handle but salvaged that situation by buying a new handle in Lidl's. Next I used a picture dictionary which I had been given by Dániel (Dáni) in the staff room. It had pages of cartoon type illustrations with each page being full of related items. The one which I used that day was pictures of stationery as I planned to, and succeeded in, buying stamps, envelopes and writing paper but couldn't find a shop holding postcards of the town's principal buildings or surrounding countryside. Then the highlight of that shopping trip was my visit to the local pharmacy. By simple universal sign language I managed to indicate to the maternal looking lady at the counter that I wished to be given a product for treating smelly feet. I just had to get her attention and then I pointed to my feet and then with my other hand took hold of my nasal passages which got the message across the language barrier in seconds. She nodded and gave a knowing smile while her assistant who was probably in her first job, having been at school till the previous summer, gave a girlish giggle which was also understandable, regardless of culture or society. Then she reached under the counter and found me a pair of Odour Eaters and a small container of Talcum powder with a particularly nice strong scent.

    As part of my contract with the school I was provided with full board for the weekdays so I then went for my evening meal at seven and had small Hungarian heavy-duty high density doughnuts. Generally speaking, the provision of full board on the weekdays is a major asset, but breakfast is supplied at what can only be considered a too early time as it's not what I'd got used to while growing up unlike the natives. I guessed I would need a good supply of energy as I had a few alterations and adjustments planned for when I got back into the flat that night.

Having tried both the beds in the flat I unfortunately concluded that the one in the study was the comfortable one and so I needed to swap it with the bedroom one. I couldn't just sleep in the study as it also had a door to the balcony and so was the coldest room in the flat without a doubt. The beds were unlike ones I'd encountered before, as the mattress was attached to the base along one side by hinges so as to provide extra storage space. Of course Murphy's Law, or as it may be in that country, Murzy's law applies. The bed I wanted to use had its hinges along the side I wanted away from the wall, so I couldn't use its space, not that I was short of storage as the hallway had built in cupboards and wardrobes. It just made it harder to tuck the sheets in. Swapping the beds from one room to the other was reminiscent of The Krypton Factor or something similar. It was physically and mentally challenging in the extreme and I was glad there wasn't a time limit. It would have been easy if the mattress and the base could be separated but they just unfolded to take up twice as much space.

Once I had completed the task I had a bath dripping in sweat in what was a very clinical appearing bathroom, done out in white tiles and cold impersonal chrome fittings. It also contained my top-loading washing machine which I would try and translate the instructions for in the next day. Lying in the bath I considered what I was told while talking to the boss man earlier. Anything I wanted or needed beyond my food and drink I was to ask them for it and they would analyse the request and grant what if any allowance they regarded necessary. I felt this would probably be a bit tiresome regarding pens, paper and other minor things but if I could persuade them what I needed was a laptop computer it could very advantageous, especially as the study has a modem in already connected.

Chapter 29

Thurs 18/9/2008. When I came to getting up the next morning, I had my first real moments of doubt of the whole trip so far. However it was just a few moments of weakness when it came to getting out of bed. This reminded me of why Dad puts his alarm clock somewhere he can't reach it from bed and so has to get out of his bed to reach the alarm clock and turn it off. This was a definite example of human nature and its lack of strength.

However I soon got over my lack of strength and was back to one hundred percent once I had a good, strong cup of Hungarian coffee. I liked the little Cafe packets I discovered there which have a combination of instant coffee, sugar and milk powder in and so just required the hot water. Ready to face the world again by the time I was downstairs waiting for my lift into the school. My first lesson was with a group of dark girls of varying heights who were well on in their studies. It was much helped by aid of textbooks which I was going to have to get myself copies of so I could do my homework. I then had a two session gap before my marathon of three lessons back to back. The first of those was with Sarah's group and just before I got started I had a phone call from my mate Mike to tell me that the love of my life, Alice was doing OK without me there for company. She was sleeping on his bed he said, which I could imagine and which was good news. That was appreciated as the next two groups were nothing like as cooperative as the dark girls group I'd already met. However in the first group there was a girl called Niki who for some reason had dropped from the above group and was very talkative in pretty good English.

Then after that was a talkative group who seemed to be following the example of their teacher. He seemed happy to use his English skills as often as possible, including socialising in the staff room. We had a good chat about words used to describe people's behaviour and character. We were finding words used to describe what is considered a good and bad personality. I practiced writing on the white board by putting up columns of what the students consider people's good and bad attributes. I was very impressed and surprised by some of the things they do and don't like and also some of the words they chose. In fact, I was so impressed by the end of the lesson that I got my phone out and used the built in camera to take some pictures of the board. That was the best lesson of the week and I thought I'd have a good time with this class and their teacher. I'd also been getting to know the Santa look alike next to my desk whose was called Josef. I discovered he had been a member of staff for years and taught just five lessons a week as he was sixty-nine years old. Music was his subject and he biked everywhere as he went to and from the school for his meals. He had a great little hobby of picking up conkers and then using his penknife to gouge out the soft inside and so leave the outer skin which he cut into a basket shape.

After school I went in town to get a radio so I could listen to World Service, but somehow I got medium rather than long wave and so didn't pick up the signal I wanted. I could get the Hungarian equivalent to Classic FM which meant it was worthwhile for then. Also I was told about an Initiation review show at the town hall put on by students who were initiating the new students, and I expected some of the sketches made reference to new teachers too. The show was at 16:00 and then after that there was a student ball at 19:00.

All the scenes were in Hungarian so the language was beyond me but some things went across the boundary such as seeing an old woman hobbling around with a shopping-bag carrying a bottle which she took swigs from every few steps as she staggered along. That was behaviour I was quite familiar with from streets in Plymouth, and I expect it's pretty universal as alcohol does seem to be. I was interested in some of the music they had for the backing music for some scenes. One had progress from Jailhouse Rock to ABBA to Black Sabbath to stuff of those days. That was all music I liked so I was glad I'd gone to the trouble of going out to the town hall and I was grateful to the lively teacher of that morning telling me about it.

On leaving the show I went on another shopping trip buying some milk powder to stock up the staff room. Also I gave in to my nicotine craving and bought a pouch of Old Holborn-esque dark baccy which was the first rolling baccy I'd found so far. There they sold it at the checkout as the sweets and chewing gum are sold in Britain. Other than that, Lidl's was about the same as it was in Plymouth or Manchester as I know from my history.

Next morning I was up in good time and the sun had risen over the horizon about the time I was getting out of bed. While I was making a cup of coffee I became aware of a hypnotising singing, chanting in the background and wandering round the flat it soon became clear it was coming from outside. I got out on to the balcony and, looking out over the green area between my block of flats and the local primary school, I soon saw there was a crowd of children standing in the morning mist singing. It was quite beautiful singing and I soon saw the kids and the accompanying teachers were being filmed. I don't know if they were recording the event for themselves for future reference or whether it was the area's local news TV show, the equivalent of Spotlight in the West Country, but there was a serious sound system provided by someone. It was such a lovely start to the day listening to these young children standing out in the mist and yet it was late enough into the day for there to be seriously hot sunshine on my face, burning up the last of the morning mist.

While I was sitting in my flat I received a delivery of assorted pieces of kitchen equipment, ranging from basic knifes to a four in one coffee machine which was capable of making espresso with high power steam. However the instructions were in Hungarian and I wasn't so keen to have a fancy frothy drink that I'd risk messing about with a steam outlet.

Once I had unpacked that, I went down to the Kollegium to use the internet and particularly see if I had a reply to the e-mail I'd sent Dad the previous evening. I had really been quite surprised by myself asking him the question I did as directly as I had. I asked him if he was proud of me and what I was doing and in the replying e-mail he said in bold print that indeed he was. I may be wrong but I'm inclined to think that his father would have been proud of him too, but I don't suppose it came up in conversation. Naval upbringing starts having an effect at a young age. One of my dad's good friends went away and started becoming a navy officer at the age of fourteen.

To try and help me to get to know the German tutors who were on a placement at the school for a month or two we were taking a day trip to Pécs which is the second biggest city of Hungary and is often regarded as the cultural capital apparently. We arrived after a reasonable length coach trip which I probably found more interesting than the others as I was still not familiar with the whole concept of travelling in an unfamiliar country. I was certainly not used to driving through large expanses of vineyards. To start with we headed for the Roman Catholic cathedral and were just in time to catch the end of the choir practicing their plainsong Gregorian chants. If I'd had a bit more cash I'd have invested in a CD of it. I think the cathedral was the most decorated place I've ever seen, with immense spreads of gilt work and painting done using the richest colours imaginable. There was also a range of stained glass windows which was quite beyond description. The other really impressive part was the bronze gates which were shaped as immense grape vines outside the wooden doors to the building. I must say that even if the Roman Catholics have a few curious ideas in the theology department, they certainly know how to decorate a place of worship. It turned out to be a real contrast as well, as later in the day we went to The Catacombs including the Seven-Apsed Sepulchral building. It is the second best old Christian painting site following Rome. It dates back to the fourth century and is now a World Heritage site.

As well as getting to know the Germans I also had the chance to get more familiar with some of the teachers who had been at Bonyhád for years. One particularly was easy to talk to, and he and his mum both taught at the school. He had done a course in teacher training or something at Pécs and so knew where to go for a good meal at a reasonable sum of Florints. It was following that meal that I made a curious discovery regarding international language phrases. Like most Hungarian restaurants and hostels, the portions were of a generous nature and, despite having finished mine and helping some of the rest of the party with theirs there was still a significant quantity of food left. I assumed we would just leave it and say "Thanks, but no thanks" to the chef. However seeing what remained on the plates the waiter came over and asked if we wished for a 'doggy bag'. Now I don't know where that expression originates but I was very surprised to hear it used so openly in a fairly high quality Hungarian eating establishment. After lunch we got back on the coach and drove off to an Adventure Park but after a brief chat with the attendant it was decided that the place was so waterlogged it wasn't really worth a visit. Luckily the staff were familiar with the local attractions and after a short consultation with the children, an adventure at the regional shopping centre was agreed on.

The local teachers obviously thought I needed to be taken out to see and do things for the first few days to help me settle in. I wouldn't have minded spending more time by myself just walking round exploring the local countryside, but I think they imagined being alone would not do me good. Being alone and loneliness are things I'd given plenty of thought to in the past and so I knew I could be in a room full of lively happy people all having a good time and yet I could feel totally alone.

As our entertainment the next day we went down the road to the slightly bigger town of Szekszárd where they were having a wine festival. Like all the towns I got to know in Hungary, entering it was like travelling through time. On the outside edge there were primitive residences which were nearly all just ground floor and I could imagine they didn't have electricity in. They had a yard round the back which had chickens or ducks in, a few vines and some veg. Often there was a pen holding a few rabbits, a goat or two which I'm sure gave milk which the ladies made into cheese and there was the family hound. I remember once I was back in Bonyhád walking round the outer edges and I was overtaken by an old man being drawn alone in a cart pulled by a shire horse. I was reminded of the rag and bone men that were just before my time back home in England. This old man had the wizened appearance of Harold Steptoe's father and I'm sure he would have given a fairly toothless grin if he had something to smile about. Maybe I was judging things wrong, but I believed for these down to earth farmers dentistry was a course of six hours, rather than years, and involved a helping of cheap vodka and a pair of rusty old pliers rather than x-rays and modern science. Yet as I often discovered, there was a serious juxtaposition of extreme opposites as listening to the clip-clop of the horse go by I watched it for a few minutes thinking about how the same style of living had been maintained in these old towns since they were first established. However when they reached the street corner they passed a T-Mobile phone box which was constructed from the leading twenty first century technology using the most advanced telecommunication systems available. However I could easily imagine the old gent and his ancestors had lived in that town for centuries and never used a telephone once. He probably had a radio but was suspicious about it. I was often curious about the road traffic in Bonyhád, as I also remember one time I was walking back to the flat after a day's teaching and coming across a man cycling towards me with a small cart in tow. I expected to find it contained a child or maybe shopping, but not. It was in fact a very self-satisfied German Shepard dog.

At the wine festival there was a concert in the church for us to attend before tasting the neighbourhood mulled wine. The music was a cross between Irish folk style and traditional pan-pipes I associated with the Andes, following Flight of the Condor. The group were a trio of a female singer that looked to be about my age, a possible boyfriend/husband on guitar and zither accompanied by an older man on pan-pipes and recorder type instrument. Quite likely they were a family that passed on the musical tradition since the middle ages. I enjoyed the sounds but I confess I found them very tranquilising so started drifting to and from consciousness. However this was a problem I had foreseen, having also suffered it in some lectures in college and occasionally on various bus and train journeys. If I was going to avoid the embarrassing event of snoring in the middle of the performance and falling off the pew as I had done from the back of a lecture theatre, I needed to quickly partake of a couple of caffeine tablets. I managed to clandestinely extract a sheet of Pro-Plus from my wallet and place two under my tongue to dissolve rapidly. They very quickly had the desired effect and I was very lively when we went and enjoyed the warm, spicy wine in the town square following the concert.

I don't know if it was always part of the plan or just due to my increased energy level, but after a plastic beaker or two of tepid red we returned to Bonyhád and joined a group of friends in their back garden for a bite to eat. They were serving local cheeses with homemade bread and green tomato relish washed down with their own produced red. There was an especially tasty salty feta type cheese. I tried not to get carried away with the wine despite it being free and very quaffable as I knew next morning I'd be in the teaching up to my neck.

Chapter 30

Every Monday morning we all assembled in the downstairs corridors of the main building which was about one hundred and fifty years old to listen to a broadcast over the PA system. I was told this was when the Head gave out significant notices and also gave the equivalent of a sermon, with some things to think about over the upcoming week. It was about 7:30 and so I heard a thought for the week in Hungarian at about the time I was used to hearing Thought for the Day in English while still in bed. Monday mornings have never been my favourite time of the week and it was the one time I had four lessons back to back without a gap. However I did usually have time for a quick roll up cigarette between each one in the staff smoking room. It was a very small dingy room which may well have never been washed out since the school was built. It reminded me of the outdoor cubicle I had used to hide in for a smoke when back at Plymouth College being a pupil rather than an educator.

I must admit to being more worried and anxious about going to face a classroom of Hungarian teenagers while working as a teaching assistant than I had been when about to face a journey of a couple of thousand miles on an Easy-Jet aeroplane. Ridiculous really, as one could potentially lead to a fatal accident whereas the others worst possible outcome was a brief period of embarrassment. As with many things, it is the anticipation that is the worst part to overcome and once engaged in the activity it is not as bad as expected. This seems to apply to numerous things such as interviews, dentist visits and teaching. It was again classes of students I hadn't dealt with before, so I started by introducing myself and telling them a bit about who I was and what I was doing there. By the end of the day I felt much more confident and I'd got the impression the students and I were just beginning to get to know each other. We would certainly have a good opportunity for that the next day as the Germans returned home at the end of that week so for 'a day off' we were all going up to Budapest the next day.

I would have liked more time in the Hungarian capital and I would still be keen to return and have a week or two to get to know it better. I could really enjoy exploring the city with a companion and so visiting the museums and galleries with someone to discuss culture with. If I was to do that my dad or S.P. would be ideal, but I'm sure I could find someone in the same category as Goldilocks or Midget to provide company, but I must admit I do doubt how far our debates on Gothic revival architecture would get. We started our school visit to the great metropolis with a visit to their parliament, which was a very classy, stylish building. It had fantastic painting all over the place but the thing which really stuck in my memory was the smoking room adjoining the main chamber. Smoking had never been allowed in the principal meeting room but as smoking seems to have always been a lead pastime in the country they had facilities for it next door. On the window sill by the linking door was a polished brass rack with numerous semi-circular dips in, it was designed for the members to leave their cigars in, smouldering away when they returned to say a few words to the house for a minute or two.

We only had time to visit one museum, and the one chosen was the National Museum of Ethnology. We also visited the Basilica and statue devoted to the national saint, Stephen. He is the man mentioned in the Christmas carol about 'Good King Wenceslas'. While we were at the gift shop I took the opportunity to buy Dad a Christmas present. I bought him a little hand painted icon, knowing he liked such things and remembering he had bought a particularly good one last time we had been to Buckfast Abbey together.

It was while we were being educated on such things that I first asked a question regarding the national badge which nobody seemed able to answer. One doesn't need to look closely at their national emblem to see it has a crown at the top which is itself topped by a cross. However the cross is not standing erect and proud, but is clearly leaning over to one side. In fact nobody seemed to be able to explain and it was thanks to Wikipedia that I got an explanation. Apparently these were the crown jewels, and at some point in history they had been stolen and hidden buried in the ground. Fortunately they were recovered, but as a symbol of Hungarian audacity and ability to recover from a low point, the damage to the crown was left as a symbol to remind the population that even if they are having a bad time they will get back to the good way things were before. Like many national flags the Hungarian is three coloured stripes. I never got round to finding out why theirs was red on white on green. However to remember it myself I told myself it was green at the bottom to represent the fertile countryside then white for the winter snow and red on that to symbolise blood spilt in their many wars to maintain freedom from the Turks and later the Soviets. Later I got the feeling from the children that they were not interested in politics and government as when I discovered the Hungarian government was a Republic none of the children could tell me what that was.

This was followed by a few days in which nothing of any note or significance occurred and then I had a day in which I had an incredible experience in the Tesco hypermarket. I was always very eager not to waste any of the limited money supply I had and so I noted down the prices of things I regularly used and compared them in the different supermarkets. I had the Aldi's and Lidl's price recorded and was walking round seeing how they matched up to Tesco's. Personally I didn't think I looked too suspicious, but obviously the store detectives didn't have the same view on things. So when after a significant length of time I eventually went to the checkout with just a couple of things in my basket they were waiting for me. I was allowed to pay for the things I had picked up but once through the checkout a couple of hefty Hungarian security guards escorted me off the main shop floor to a little office where a manager of some sort was awaiting me. Unfortunately they didn't seem to have a single member of staff capable of speaking English, so by sign language they explained to me they thought I had been shoplifting and so wished to search me for illegally obtained goods. I had no idea what rights I had regarding resisting their plans or what they legally had permission to do if I decided to resist them. Having been strip searched in the past I didn't feel that if they went that far they would causing irreparable damage to my personal dignity as that had occurred years ago. Therefore I chose not to struggle too much as I was definitely in a position where they had the upper hand, and it was quite possible the large Hungarian mountains of humanity whom I faced had been trained by men who had done that kind of physical work for the Soviets if not actually done it themselves.

Luckily in fact they just wanted me to remove my big black leather overcoat and get down to my under garments which couldn't conceal anything of any significance or value. That was quite a reasonable request really as in the past I'd managed to fit a three litre bottle of white cider in the inside pocket of that coat and then walk around without it being at all obvious from the outside. My wallet was also examined by a small man who I felt was the brains of the operation, maybe trying out his powers as a deputy manager while the proper one was away. He was sat at a table which reminded me of the chair and table arrangement I knew well from police interview rooms witnessed personally in reality and on A Touch of Frost and similar. He started filling in the details of a report sheet which was clearly the Hungarian version of an international Tesco piece of paperwork. First he put in the time and date which appear the same whatever country it is for, then his and the store's details. To find out my different facts and figures he looked through the assorted plastic cards I had with me. Before coming out to Hungary I had been very careful to ensure I had a European Health Insurance Card with me and maybe he recognised the EU symbol of the circle of stars and so felt he could trust the information on there. Unfortunately he copied the information down incorrectly so Tesco received a report on a suspicious character in the Bonyhád store with the surname: Jamesgeorge. I can't really say why but I've never liked Tesco as a brand and that afternoon's experience certainly didn't improve my view of them, so I only use them in times of serious desperation.

Still, I managed to leave the store after a considerable delay and was no worse off than I had been. It seemed more than likely if I'd had a similar experience a few years previously I'd have ended up in the gulag, so I was content to leave things as they were and do all my shopping in Aldi and Lidl unless it was essential I went to Tesco.

Back home I had picked up a considerable number of quality possessions which I confess I found either out in the street or awaiting disposal in one way or another. For example I've a large impressive picture in my flat's front room which portrays what I think is either a Norwegian fjord or a scene in the wilds of Canada which I found in a skip waiting to be taken to Chelson Meadow, the Plymouth landfill site. I therefore had no inhibitions about picking up a small saucepan which I found out in the streets when I was walking home, still in somewhat of a state of shock that evening. I was taking a slow indirect route home as it was a lovely clear night with numerous bats flying around in the air. It reminded me of an event I had persuaded my dad to join me for in which one evening we met up with a crowd of other nature lovers to walk beside a river on the edge of Dartmoor for a 'Moths and Bats' walk. The best part of it had been standing beside the river and watching the bats dive down out of nowhere to skim over the water surface to have a little sip to drink of the beautiful clear water.

The next morning I received my first postage after struggling to confirm what my Hungarian postal address was and also needing to get hold of a key to allow me entry to my post box just inside the hall on the ground floor of the block of flats in which I was residing. I was very surprised that my first letter came from some I knew from Stoke Damerel Bible Study and as the weeks went by some people impressed me while others left me quite disgruntled with their frequency of correspondence. I didn't find contact with friends and family so essential to maintain my high spirits as I had when I was at Portland. I was disappointed when I'd asked for pictures of Plymouth and Dartmoor to use to decorate my flat walls and also to show to the students when describing where I lived yet received none.

When introducing myself to another class one student particularly impressed me when we were talking about poetry reading. He said he was very keen on poems especially those of Robert Burns and Lord Byron.

Chapter 31

I was very glad to have left behind all the intricacies and elaborate relationships my friends at Plymouth engaged in. I regularly told them and people at the writing groups I didn't need to watch soap operas, I got more than enough of that type of entertainment just observing all the ploys and plots of my various drinking partners. Worst of all was the girl I had known for years who considered me to be her brother as I never tried it on with her. Struggling to be a Good Samaritan I would regularly let her stay at mine for a night or two when she had split up with her current boyfriend. She had a choice of three companions she would flit between depending on whose pay day it was and how much they had managed to keep their alcoholic abuse in check. As I have seen is often the case with domestic violence, she knew none of them were constructive worthwhile relationships but as long as they provided her with cheap cider, tobacco and taxis she would tow the line.

I used to hate the situations she would get me into as what regularly happened was things would be quiet and peaceful for a few weeks then at about 10:30pm I'd receive a text asking me to phone her back asap. I knew what would be about to happen but my ideas of Christian charity meant I couldn't refuse the request. So when I rang she answered in a plaintive sorrowful voice saying she had no money till next morning and she had just had a row with X resulting in her having to lock herself in the bathroom for protection and then call out the police. They knew the address and names very well, but nobody ever maintained charges and so after a night or two at mine then maybe an interlude with an alternative boyfriend she returned to where she had to escape from previously, convinced things would change for the better this time. One thing which made it an unfathomably difficult situation to resolve was the housing arrangements.

For a while she had a relationship with a man who had a comfortable pension from working in the dockyard for about twenty years and so was receiving cash via that and like most people in that Plymouth soap was also claiming benefits from the government in what seemed excessive amounts to me. I was the only one on Job Seekers Allowance as they all got Incapacity benefit, Income Support or something similar and they couldn't understand why I didn't do the same. This was just another example of how in my mind justice is something which was really in short supply in the UK. So the two of them lived in a flat which was in her name, but when his behaviour became intolerable she had packed a few things in a bag and gone to stay with another friend. Therefore he was in her flat but as long as she got about forty pounds off him a week she was happy to leave things like that. However when the supplier of an alternative roof over her head let the standards of his conduct slip she couldn't stay where she had been or return to her flat. She would usually turn up on her own doorstep physically and emotionally drained without her keys and persuade him to let her back in exchange for a quantity of alcohol and tobacco. I've lost count of how many times she has said to me she'd go back to her flat with the police and so have him kicked out followed by a change of the locks. I can only put it down to her being a sad spineless alcoholic as all he had to do was turn on the charm and the drink supply and she would give him a couple more weeks in which to find himself somewhere else to reside. That gave him time to get another cheque in and so give her a wad of cash so she could drown her sorrows again.

As if this wasn't enough trouble in her life, she also had children that lived a few hours train journey away staying with other members of her family. She planned to go and visit them about once a month but there was one she hadn't seen for over fifteen years, one she was getting back with after a few years apart and one who she had maintained contact with. If she had a heavy drinking session the night before she either missed the train or caught it but turned up in a pretty washed out state having eaten little if anything over the past weeks and having consumed nothing except cheap white cider tinted with blackcurrant squash and some instant cappuccino coffees.

What makes it all so terrible is that while I was at Plymouth doing my degree and then the TEFL course I had known a lady whose drinking got heavier and heavier from bottles of Lambrini every few days to a couple of bottles of vodka a day via white cider and Special Brew strength lagers. I could then and still can now see a pattern slowly but horribly repeating itself. In fact that lady died just a few days before I returned to Plymouth for Christmas and so I was just back in time to attend her funeral.

While in Hungary I discovered some curious food stuffs at their restaurants and also in the shopping establishments and supermarkets. If I could have read Hungarian I probably would have found even more. I remember when we visited a town market and one stall had huge glass tanks packed full of fish still swimming around. I was surprised but thinking about it later it made sense and I don't know why we don't do the same here. To some extent we do, as in the good restaurants, and I've done it once, the customer can pick a lobster and in our Plymouth market the seafood stall has crabs lying on their backs waving their brittle armour plated legs in the air.

A couple of other non-English food stuffs I noticed were at a meat counter at which one could buy chicken feet, which I assumed were used for making stock and there were also turkey hearts which I used in a stir fry but, like chicken's liver was meant for a pate type dish. These days, back in Plymouth, a number of shops have opened up to cater for our horde of Polish and other Eastern European taxi drivers. These store's provisions include numerous spice mixes, unfamiliar vegetables and tins of octopus arms in their midst. Following my time in Hungary I now add celeriac, kohlrabi, okra and Chinese leaves to my range of vegetables. I do sympathise with the local children who are still working on pronunciation and so seeing a store with "The Polish Shop" over the door ask their mum why we need a whole shop to supply polish, not realising it sounds like Poe-lish in its shopping context. I also discovered a great supply of carbohydrate to add to my directory while eating meals provided for me at the school. I had never had Bulgar cracked wheat with a stew or goulash previously but now I often have it either as a sponge to soak up sauce/gravy with a main course, or mixed in salad similarly to couscous. It certainly suits me sometimes as it is so easy, one just leaves it soaking in boiled water for half an hour and then it is ready for use. Another accompaniment for goulash type meals which I didn't really know of previously is soured cream which, like Greek yoghurt, adds smoothness to a dish. In the school canteen there were the usual salt and pepper containers but there was also a little dish of dried red chillies which some people crumbled into their soup or stew. I picked a couple one lunch time to take back and add to the dish I was doing that evening. However I was distracted while adding them, by a phone call I think and it resulted in me forgetting I'd been handling them and so foolishly I rubbed my eyes after handling the chillies. When I had been away at one of our army camps as a cadet I had been exposed to CS gas after we were forced to take off our gas masks in a test facility, and that was about the most similar experience I was aware of before getting chilli in my eyes. It gave me an idea of what pepper spray is probably like.

Apart from cookery I have a couple of ways of entertaining myself while in my flat in Bonyhád. I use my mobile phone to connect to the internet and so I used Red Hot Pawn.com which is an international chess playing website, and because I enjoy playing games I'm also signed up to the Diplomacy website. To inform those who don't know, Diplomacy is a board game set in Europe at the start of the twentieth century. It has seven players each representing a European country or empire and what makes it so interesting is that the players discuss with each other who they plan to help and who they with gang up against. It is all about getting people to trust you and then support your attacks till you can make an alliance with someone else and so stab your previous ally in the back. It is ideal for play on the internet as then nobody knows who is talking with each other and people who can't lie very well face to face can still make up deceptions and mislead other rulers.

Once I found the town's library I had another way to pass the time, though they only had a small selection of books in English. These were an interesting range as they included a Stephen King novel, a Jane Austen, a copy of "The Silence of the Lambs" and a great anthology of Hungarian poetry. I was so impressed by modern Hungarian poetry that I used Amazon to buy a copy of the modern anthology "The Colonnade of Teeth" and when I left the staff gave me a book of poems by Milán Füst who also wrote plays and a novel. Despite winning awards and being short listed for the Nobel literature prize if a Hungarian is asked to name the top ten poets of the nation he is unlikely to be mentioned.

I got the impression that teenagers can be divided into the same sort of categories regardless of which country they are in and also irrespective of time period. As I got to know my students I was particularly reminded of the film "The Breakfast Club" in which there is a brain, an athlete, a basket case, a princess and a rebel. As I got to know one of the brains I discovered he was a geek and so I got him to help me with the computers. I agreed with the staff to do a talk once every two weeks on a subject I knew about and the students had no knowledge of. The best ones I did were on the history of Plymouth, history of England and poetry structures. My geek friend was very helpful for the first couple as he knew how to take pictures from Wikipedia which had a copyright and then download them on to a memory stick so I could include them in the PowerPoint presentation I gave via the laptop I borrowed from the Head of the English department and connected to a projector. Thus I showed pictures of Plymouth, its famous sons such as Tobias Fernaux (first man to circumvent the world in both directions and buried in the cemetery of my local church) and English Kings and Queens.

The poetry presentation looked at sonnets, rhyming couplets, haikus, quatrains and limericks among other things. I used the limericks to show the students how easily poems could be written as I wrote them a couple about the school, myself and other things they could relate to on demand while standing at the front of the class. Also because a lot of them had the idea that poetry was very complicated, wordy and hard to understand, even for somebody whose native language it was in and that had studied it to degree level I introduced them to some of Ogden Nash's masterpieces such as The Fly. 'God in his wisdom made the fly, and then forgot to tell us why.'

I had a few interesting experiences on days out, in which this time we went to some local tourist attractions rather than having a long coach trip to a big city. I don't know if the students thought less of it because we didn't go so far but I certainly enjoyed it, yet that was partly due to where we went and what we saw, but also I had interesting, enlightening chats with a few students during the journey. One that I particularly recall was a girl called Rebeka sitting next to me and talking about taste in music. She was a very pretty girl with all the soft pink feminine touches such as fingernails, make up, perfume, a handbag and all the other things I was completely unfamiliar with. Yet we soon found out we liked the same kind of music as I showed her what I had on the memory card of my phone and she recognised bands such as Iron Maiden, Slayer and Marilyn Manson. As we had about three quarters of an hour on the bus she had the chance to listen to a song or two of Pitchshifter, Ministry, Nine Inch Nails, and Black Sabbath, all of which she enjoyed and I gave a few other names to feed in to a search engine when given the chance. So a week or two later she gave me a CD of a local band she had copied for me in return for introducing her to Cradle of Filth, Rage against the Machine, Hellbastard and Lawnmower Deth. Definitely another case of not judging a book by its cover as I confess I thought she looked as if she would have found Madonna, Kylie Minogue and Pink rather heavy duty, but in fact she liked the bands who promote themselves with tee-shirts that have "Jesus is a cunt" written on them.

After that interesting discussion about musical taste we arrived at a castle and in the next few hours I encountered a few things which left a number of permanent images in my mind following my visit to Hungary. The castle had been a defence point against the Turks and had seen active service on a number of occasions. It still had cannon balls embedded in the walls from when the Turks had last put it under siege. I don't know why but there was something very tangible and in your face about seeing a stone wall inches thick with a solid sphere of iron entrenched in it. Then, inside the castle we had various displays showing its history including portraits of its previous owners looking down on the dining hall. In an upstairs couple of rooms there was an exhibition of modern art works including an especially good picture- 'nude with a mobile' which just seemed to be such a contrast to the men's' portraits downstairs.

Following our packed lunch we spent the afternoon on a boat trip along a tributary of the Danube. I picked up a few of the more interesting coloured or shaped pebbles off the beach so I could give them to friends of mine back home and tell them they were stones from the Danube. A cheap way to give someone a souvenir which is authentic from Hungary but not a rip off purchased at a gift shop. We followed that by a wander round a wildlife park which apparently had wild boar, wolves and possibly even a bear or two ranging around in it but we never saw any of those. What we did see however was a young deer. It was by itself in a paddock as its mother had rejected it or been eaten by a bear or something. The group of kids I was with and I expected it to run a mile on our appearance despite the link and chain fence between us and it. However it slowly meandered up to us and in fact pushed its nose through the fence to try and suckle from the knee of my trousers. What made this particularly surprising was that I was wearing my Disruptive Pattern Material ones in red, white and black.

Chapter 32

As the next day was a Sunday I decided to go down to the local church and see what kind of a reception I'd receive. Clearly the Roman Catholic faith has been a very significant thing in the history of the town as in its centre was a town square which was surrounding a church on the island in the middle. It had clearly been there for a few hundred years and also it had been refurbished recently. I had been to the Roman Catholic cathedral in Plymouth a few times to attend a Bach Mass and also a version of the Stations of the Cross service. They were probably the most uncomfortable pews I knew in England but they were quite luxurious in relation to the Hungarian ones. Whoever designed these had obviously been thinking of the devotees who used to torture themselves by self-whipping and here they inflicted pain by just sitting in the pews.

I kept track of the service on the sheet as best I could despite having already reached the conclusion that Hungarian was a very difficult language to follow. Luckily I managed to find a couple of bits at which I could join in, such as a part where the priest announced a phrase and we the congregation called out "Hallelujah, hallelujah" in reply. I had expected that as ever since I had been a teenage altar boy and especially later I would go up to members of the clergy and especially lay readers in training and ask them what things such as 'Hallelujah' or 'Hosanna' meant. I must admit I have been in church congregations where I suspect half the members don't actually know what they are saying when they use such words. That's why I think people like William Tyndale did so much for the English population in the time of the Reformation. Translating the Bible out of Greek and Hebrew into a form the everyday man in the street could read and comprehend. One thing which I found unbelievably surprising about the Holy Communion service was that we went up to the priest and we were all given our piece of cardboard wafer but there was no wine for anyone except the clergy. Now I must admit I didn't mind that for a couple of reasons. Principally that I think communion wine tastes disgusting anyway, but also as a secondary reason ever since my time in rehab I don't take communion wine as it means every Sunday I reflect while others are taking theirs, on all the misery I have seen or heard of which alcohol is responsible for. Unfortunately I'm still very aware of it too, as recently I was visited by a "friend of mine" who, due to her being an alcoholic, had been thrown out of her flat and so had nobody else to stay with on a cold February night. However, because I had no money to go and buy her some drink for that night she left my place after midnight having had a confrontation with police officers who were already very familiar with her and her reputation. She had been with her previous boyfriend before for about two and a half years. I've got the impression from watching her and other people that that is about the average length a relationship lasts before one of them being an alcoholic destroys it and results in it all falling apart. The other night this "friend of mine" at last got confronted by the harsh reality of life and people finally stood up to her and said they could take no more of her lying, playing them off against each other and being more devoted to her supply of alcohol than to the person supposed her partner. It had been on the horizon for a long time, slowly getting closer and closer, more inevitable and then it happened the other night. It made me think, as she kept trying to call different friends with it becoming more and more obvious they weren't going to answer her pleas for money to buy alcohol with. I'm sure some of them had traded sexual favours for alcohol supplies in the past, but even that had finally worn out. This was so little bit by bit that it occurred to me as we broke up our dogends to make a last desperate hit of nicotine from the cigarettes which had had already been recycled twice so these were the dogends of dogends. I concluded that the brutal harsh reality of life generally has its effect on people in one of two ways. Either it smashes them in the face out of the blue as had happened with me and my mum's car accident, or it wears them down similar to the erosion of sandstone by rainwater. This also has a very strong effect as can be seen in the Grand Canyon or Cheddar Gorge in England but it's a slow grinding, relentless unperceivable yet unavoidable effect. This was the effect alcohol has and it's very similar to the spread of cancer which killed my friend Mike's wife over months and months.

When in Hungary, as I expected, I had plenty of time for reading and writing as I only got two TV channels which transmitted in English. One I watched every morning over breakfast to find out what was happening in the world, CNN. The other had a curious range of programs and assorted times and was called BBC Prime. I got the impression it transmitted with the aim of entertaining ex-patriots in Europe rather than providing amusement and information for Europeans that had learnt to speak and understand English. It was heavily loaded with sitcoms which I enjoyed but I don't know if such things would appeal to non-English senses of humour. For example we regularly got Blackadder, Red Dwarf, The Vicar of Dibley and a really good one I don't remember having seen at home called Suburban Shootout.

On my next day off I decided to take another trip to the cultural hotspot of Pécs and explore it at my own rate with a number of Forint in my pocket. I particularly remember finding a sizable quality bookshop with a considerable English section in. I was fascinated to see which books they had in stock. There were three sections; classics, modern classics and anything else. Thus I could find Jane Austen, Daniel Defoe, Brontë sisters and Dickens as World Classics while William Golding, Graham Greene and Salman Rushdie were Modern Classics. In the remaining section which contained numerous best sellers and was similar to the book rack I dealt with at Luton airport when I returned home a number of weeks later. Irvin Walsh, John Grisham, Anne Rice, Mills and Boon assorted and the like filled that shelf. I'm not sure but I think there was a section for Russian classics such as Tolstoy, Dostoyevsky and Solzhenitsyn. I was never really sure quite how the Hungarians felt about the Soviets, having only regained their freedom within the last generation. Surely some members of the society such as Josef who sat next to me in the staffroom had bad memories and could even just remember back before the war.

Having browsed the bookshop I was very curious as to what a book had to do to be defined as a 'classic'. Surely a date could be selected and before or after that would decide if it was a modern one or not. I'm not sure but I think an antique is defined by its age as it has to be over one hundred years old to be so. In a similar sort of vein I'm fascinated that legally *time immemorial* is defined by statute as 1189. If our church at Stoke Damerel were just a couple of decades older it would have been around since time immemorial. I think, because I am helped to feel comfortable by things I've been familiar with in the past that was one reason I had peanut butter on my list of things to look for while in the city centre having, been unable to find it in any supermarket in Bonyhád. Music I'm familiar with is also a very reassuring thing, and I was glad I'd spent time loading up my phone's memory cards with albums. Yet I took advantage of a very Gothic type store to browse their CD collection. I nearly bought an album by Ministry which had a clever title by my reckoning. Namely "*Dark side of the Spoon*". Obviously a pun on the famous Pink Floyd '*Dark side of the Moon*' yet also a reminder that a teaspoon is heated by a cigarette lighter or a candle flame to 'cook up' a heroin hit and so is soon coated in soot. I chose not to buy the album eventually but did take the opportunity to buy a black tee-shirt. On the front was the Hungarian emblem being held up by an angel, clearly displaying the intriguing crooked cross. Upon the back of the tee-shirt the modern political Hungarian map being pulled in five roughly equal sized pieces by clutching hands. Quite what, if anything, this represented I was unsure but it was enough for me to show people back home where I had been in relation to Budapest and the largest European lake. Unfortunately I never had a chance to visit Lake Balaton. One of the other TEFL teachers I had met at Budapest, the older lady who was the one I could get on with as she didn't strike me as a school kid herself, unlike the rest of them, was posted to a school near the lake.

I did buy some music however as I went back for another look at the breath taking cathedral and had a look around in the crypt on that trip too. Following my visit and as a sort of contribution to their fund for maintaining the beautiful artwork so rife in and around the building I visited the gift shop where I got a small hand painted icon which I knew I could give my dad as a Christmas gift. This time I got a CD of Sacred Voice which is quite hypnotic Hungarian religious chanting that is similar to Hildegard of Bingen.

When I returned to Bonyhád I got off the bus outside the town library for a couple of reasons. Firstly because I needed to find myself a new book to read and also because it was about five o'clock and so dusk, which is my favourite time of day. This was a good time to go and visit the library as it was in its own little park in which there was a fountain made from a brass horse sculpture and that was surrounded by benches to sit on and read books. Also the park had resident black squirrels that were very nervous, quite possibly because they were on the menu there. I didn't realise it at the time but in *The Joy of Cooking* which I had a copy of back in Plymouth I had a recipe to do them. I imagine they would be similar to rabbit but even bonier. At that time of year it was terrific to sit in the park and read something like *Eragon* which was what I had out then. It is the first book in a trilogy about a dragon and its rider. The trees were at the peak of their autumnal colours at the time and I imagine were about as impressive as the famous Appalachians leaf colours.

The first few weeks of being a teacher living in Hungary working in a school very reminiscent of the one I'd gone to myself was basically OK. I had no trouble with the food as I'll eat just about anything and apart from when I fell asleep on the flat's sofa watching Red Dwarf after a few glasses of wine and I burnt a hole in it as I dropped my roll up my home life was fine. The only other problem I ever really encountered while in the flat was when I slipped with a knife in the kitchen and nearly removed the end of my left index finger. If the cut had been any worse I would have had to find out how to get to the nearest Accident and Emergency to get a few stiches which would have been very difficult. Hard to explain using language what I wanted but considering the quantity of blood I was losing I could make it pretty clear by sign language, what exactly my problem was.

Sometimes as I was walking into the school in the morning I found it hard to believe that all this was actually happening. I really was in a small town in Eastern Europe teaching English. At last I was doing something worthwhile with my life and it made my dad proud. We had classes just after half term which I think he would have been particularly impressed by. The subject for the week was the local world/the environment, and by the end of it we were talking about recycling which I didn't think was an especially big issue in Hungary. However by the time we had finished talking about it I really got the impression the students felt guilty for all the litter they had dropped and they wished they had recycled their glass bottles. There was a bottle bank in the town centre and I think it got a flood of deliveries for a couple of weeks after that. However with a lot of things, especially for people like teenagers it isn't starting things that are difficult it is maintaining them.

I was introduced to the school library eventually and the reason was not directly connected to their literature. It was because that was the room in which they had a scanner that was linked to a computer. I wanted to use that as I had an e-mail from my fellow TEFL teacher at Lake Balaton saying she was having trouble with her prepositions. I had a few text books with me and I thought one of them was especially good at explaining that area so I sent her a copy of the relevant chapter. I also sent her a little poem it contained.

The Old Fashioned Rules of Grammar

A Noun's the name of any thing
As *school,* or *garden, hoop* or *swing.*

Adjectives describe the kind of noun
As *great, small, pretty, white* or *brown.*

Instead of nouns the Pronouns fit-
As *he, you, they* and *it.*

Verbs tell of something being done-

To *read, write, count, sing, jump* or *run*.

How, when and where the Adverbs tell,
As *slowly, near ,now* or *well*.

Conjunctions join the words together,
As men *and* women, wind *or* weather.

The prepositions stands before
A Noun as *in* or *through* a door.

The interjection shows surprise,
As *Oh,* how pretty, *Ah,* how wise.

Three little words you often see,
Are Articles *a, an* and *the*.

One teacher I got on particularly well with was called Zarah and we started off having talks in the teacher's smoking room. Smoking maybe very bad for one's health but it can be a terrific ice-breaker in certain social situations, crossing barriers of age, gender and nationality. It resulted eventually with my visiting her home as we helped each other in a couple of ways. As well as teaching she also worked part-time doing translations of legal documents and other technical pieces with numerous complex words and ideas. One I particularly remember was an instruction manual for a home cinema system. I would read through her translation to just see if it read easily and occasionally did what I could to explain concepts. In return she recommended and lent text books, gave me a meal at her house and showed me that Hungary was not a totally cat-free society.

By then I'd read *Eragon* and was now trying to get through what I'd call another heavy duty classic. These are things such as *War and Peace, Don Quixote, Brothers Karamazov* and in this case *The Hunchback of Notre Dame*. In these tomes it can be incredible how much description can be given, especially to a place. I can't recall if it was *Ulysses* or *The Portrait of the Artist as a Young Man* but in one James Joyce gives a fantastic detailed description of hell. However Victor Hugo gave me seventy pages of Paris using hard wearing language. It must be a personality characteristic but once I've started something I don't like to stop part way through. I'm much happier getting to the end. This applies to everything from smoking a cigarette or listening to a song up to reading a trilogy. Because of this I was very reluctant to quit the hunchback's story but I did and so took up a regular modern page turner. I found Bonyhád library had *Desperation* by Stephen King. I hadn't read anything by him for years but I had enjoyed *Pet Sematary* when I was at school. One thing which always comes to mind when Stephen King is mentioned is a great character. Not one in a book of his but someone from a Plymouth writers group. She is an elderly lady who has all Stephen King books on her home shelves and is very familiar with James Herbert and numerous other horror writers. When I first met her she looked as if she would be straight into a discussion of Jane Austen but instead she asked who my favourite Gothic/horror writer was. She talked with more use of expletives than I often heard while talking to retired Royal Marines or dockyard workers. When I told her I liked H.P. Lovecraft that was OK by her standards but a bit low on blood and guts, being from the early twentieth century.

I don't know why but one morning I woke up and really didn't feel very well at all. When at home in Plymouth I could usually put it down to my alcohol consumption the previous evening but obviously that wasn't the case this time. I felt so bad that I wrote in my diary that I felt like a spider crab. Now of course I shouldn't be so presumptuous as to assume that spider crabs don't feel good just because of how they appear to me. Maybe all crustaceans feel fantastic. I think lobsters dance a quadrille in some situation, so I expect they feel good doing that.

Back in Plymouth I don't know any teenagers very well and so my ideas regarding them as a social group were probably very influenced by Eastenders, news programs and talks with people who have them as their own children. I certainly have got the impression from somewhere that the majority of them are obese, alcoholics who are being mentally and emotionally damaged by computer games and the internet. One thing I think the British kids could learn about from the ones there is regarding eating habits. The kids at the school are frequently munching things but there it's sunflower seeds and assorted nuts rather than chocolate and other artificial sweet substances. The whole lifestyle seems healthier in general, but I don't know if that's due to being in Hungary or being in the countryside. Most families grow their own fruit and vegetables and often have their own vineyards from which they produce a home-made wine. I noticed that when eating grapes with seeds they nearly always ate the seeds too.

One good evening the English teachers were invited to reassemble in the staff room at about six in the evening on a Friday to partake of a tasting session. This was as one teacher's family had an especially good reputation for producing their own wine so it had become a tradition to have a get together when the first bottles of a particular crop when opened. Now wine is one of many things I wish I knew more about, and I got the suspicion that growing up in an environment in which it is so involved it becomes second nature. I certainly enjoyed the bus journeys I took from Bonyhád to other local towns which took us past vineyards on a scale I was completely unfamiliar with. Yet walking through the streets to soak up the Hungarian atmosphere in Bonyhad at the weekends I often saw vines in people's gardens.

One major difference in culture I'm very aware of here and now is the significance of Christmas. In England, Christmas's approach becomes obvious from any time after Halloween and Bonfire Night. When I was just a week or so away from Christmas I don't think I'd have known it if I hadn't been shopping in Aldi's and Lidl's as they had the same Christmas cards and chocolates there as in Plymouth, just not so promoted. In a lot of our English lessons previously we had been looking at the cultural diversity and difference for various family events such as birthdays, marriages and name days there. We had been examining the differences in national events such as differences in what the English and the Hungarians do at Christmas, St Nicholas's day and I explained about the fifth of November and Guy Fawkes. I also got some of the more advanced students to explain to me what a republic is as that is the Hungarian governmental system.

I did some Hungarian Christmas shopping over my last few days and I confess I was quite happy to ignore its approach for as long as possible as I get seriously fed up with the length of time it dominates everything in the UK. Another thing which contributes to it annoying me is that some of my favourite hymns are Advent ones including *O Come, o come Emmanuel* which is my favourite of all time. I think it has some very strong imagery in the lyrics and I remember rehearsing it at prep school with the wild music teacher and I think that ingrained it into my musical memory. As a present for Dad I bought a bottle of Hungary's national drink 'Unicum'. I'd no idea what it tasted like but from what I'd been told and read in various places including Wikipedia I suspected it was rather a bitter, herbal brew.

As a school tradition we all went to the local Lutheran church on the term's penultimate evening for a very laid back, chilled out evening service by candlelight. It's surprising how much pleasure you can get from a service or a concert even when you don't know what the people are saying. I suppose I should have realised that from the operas Aunt used to take Dad and me to. After the first couple the Theatre Royal had a system for superscripts as they called it. A screen above the stage had a translation of the words projected on. It was in such a position to certainly discourage sitting 'up in the gods' as it was only partially visible from there. After the service we returned to the school hall for a sort of goodbye Christmas party. It was another quite subdued affair with quiet seasonal music in the background, plenty of wine consumed by staff and students in sensible quantities due to the national culture. People generally used it as an occasion to say goodbye and share cakes, biscuits and garnished wafers. I said farewell to all the other English teachers but particularly found it a fine time to talk to the school cook. He was a hearty Hungarian gent who I'd introduced myself to early in my stay. There had been a number of occasions I had turned up for a meal after everyone else had been and gone yet he hadn't seen me in the canteen and so a good plate of goulash was put back for me. He also quickly discovered my favourite meals and allowed me to have seconds on those days. When we went on day trips we were given packed lunches and I regularly found an extra chocolate biscuit or piece of cold pizza in mine. He was clearly another reason for me to vouch for Hungarian hospitality.

Chapter 33

My baggage was heavy enough when I arrived and it was even worse leaving as I had more books, enough to fill all my hand luggage and I had a couple of bottles and some Christmas gifts. It was lucky they only weighed my bags and not me as I was wearing about four layers of clothing under my black leather overcoat and every pocket was crammed with assorted items. I got prearranged lifts from the flat to the school and then after leaving some tea, coffee, biscuits and having a last cigarette with Zarah, which was the closest moment to an emotional goodbye I got, I took another ride to the town bus station. A number of students were already there as they were on their way across the country to get home. Some just up the road, some to Budapest and some for hundreds of miles to the east. Mostly they were ones I recognised but didn't really know as they were in other classes but there was also Niki who was one of my favourites who I'd had some interesting conversations with about music and fashion.

The bus to Szekszárd which was where I was supposed to change for my Budapest bus had been due to arrive at 14:20. I must confess I got just a bit anxious when it still hadn't turned up by 14:40. I bought bus tickets on demand but had booked and paid for my flight and a coach to Plymouth so I didn't want to miss any connections. Then a bus to Szekszárd turned up but was full and took on no passengers which had me break out into a bit of a sweat. I asked Niki what was going on as she was about the only person I could talk to. She asked at the office and found that due to other colleges and educational establishments shutting up there was a flood of students that day. However another bus was laid on and was going to turn up in ten minutes or so. I breathed a discernible sigh of relief had a cigarette with Niki and then got on a bus to Szekszárd. Despite trying to resist I soon feel asleep on the bus but I was lucky enough to wake up about half an hour later where I recognised the outskirts of Szekszárd and so took a couple of Pro Plus caffeine tablets to avoid going back to sleep and missing the change as I had done in the past. I clearly remember one time I was on a train and was meant to change at Westbury yet I fell asleep and just as I regained consciousness I looked out the window and saw the Westbury station sign going past as we pulled out of the station.

After a three quarters of an hour wait over a couple of coffees and some quality dark chocolate biscuits I boarded my Budapest coach. That journey terminated in the big city so sleep was acceptable then and of course due to my tablets and coffees I couldn't relax on that trip. However it meant I was awake to see my final Hungarian sunset over the mountains which was more than satisfactory. It was dark by the time I unloaded at Budapest and so I made straight for the nearest taxi rank. I don't know what percentage of the taxi drivers spoke English but luckily I found one that did as I overheard a few Germans leaving him. It turned out to be fortunate as on arrival at the airport we found the terminal I was expecting to use had no staff present and was all locked up. Thanks to being able to talk to my taxi driver I soon established it was a strike or something but my flight was still on a little later than expected at the secondary terminal.

I don't know now and didn't know then quite what the laws and rules are about taking liquids on flights but I got the impression I could take a bottle if they didn't know about it. The bottle of Unicum I had for Dad was buried in my suitcase and so it was alright, but I had been given a bottle of rosé by the college staff on departure and so that was quite prominent being on top of everything else. As I still had a bit of time in hand I consumed as much of it as I could over my last nicotine hit till I landed at Luton. I then checked in at the Easy-Jet desk and, after discussing things with a friendly attendant decided to throw away a heavy spacious jigsaw puzzle I had also been given on leaving and I paid a little extra for excess luggage if I remember rightly.

I then went through and spent almost the last of my Forints in duty free buying a hundred Lucky Strike cigarettes for one friend as I promised I would. This was in return to what she gave me once a month or so as she had connections with army logistics and supplied me with large quantities of instant coffee, sugar and cereals. I also got a bottle of quality Cognac for Paul as a Christmas present I knew he would share with me. To fill in the time till boarding I went through to the lounge for a relaxed cigarette and a pint of Stella. I met an interesting crowd of Greeks there that were returning home after an educational trip to Budapest. We started our conversation when I told them I'd originally planned to go to Greece but missed the chance as I was late letting it be known. Once the ice was broken at least one of the Greek girls was quite happy to make what I would have considered some personal comments to me. We had only been talking for a few minutes when she twitched her nose, looked at me quizzically and told me I smelt like an artist. I told her if that included writers then I suppose she was correct. She told me she was a painter and I told her I painted pictures using words. We had a chat for a while about what defines art and artists until I was called to board my flight on which I got a seat at the back of the plane by a window.

I flew out in daytime and this was a night flight which gave me the chance to see all the illuminated towns and cities which was an interesting contrast to previous views. I enjoy flying, except that it was agonising to my eardrums as we came in to land at Luton at 23:00. I then had seven hours to fill before catching a coach to Heathrow where I was to change and get the one back to home sweet home, Plymouth. I had only been away for a few months but I had forgotten how foolish English people could be when under the influence of alcohol. I met a couple in the lounge that were also waiting for transport. He was ranting and raving about an encounter he had just had out the front as he had gone for a stroll to get some fresh air and pass the time. He had met a young man out there who asked him for a cigarette. For some reason this had caused offence and so now he was back with his partner he was telling her how he felt like tearing the young man's head off and shitting down his neck. From the tired expression on her face I got the impression she was all too familiar with such encounters and had had it to the back teeth. She definitely had a look of long suffering ground into her face.

The security guard had clearly been aware of the couple for a while but decided to keep a discreet distance till Mr Antisocial moved on to a different subject. He started pointing to some unaccompanied baggage and shouting about terrorists, bombs and 9/11. I quickly told him they were mine and the guard told me to keep them in my view all the time I remained on site. This provoked the ranter to say to his companion that I was clearly using my loaf. I found this amusing as I had already reached the conclusion I thought that he was a total idiot whatever he thought about me. Looking at my mobile phone I saw I was almost out of battery power and so I found a socket beside a chair so I sat down and tried recharging my phone for free. Clearly the airport had anticipated this as there was no power at the socket and a cleaner seeing what I was doing told me they only got powered up when being used for vacuum cleaners or other similar equipment.

To pass the time I then went and browsed the airport literature in WHSmith. I hadn't particularly planned to buy a book, just see what was among the bestsellers at the time and then maybe buy a newspaper to catch up on life in Great Britain. However I found a book by unknown author Heather O'Neill called *Lullabies for Little Criminals* which in the blurb on the back had a quote from TLS comparing Baby, the book's main character to Holden Caulfield from *Catcher in the Rye*. As that was a book I particularly enjoyed both times I read it I chose to splash out and invest in Miss O'Neill. Also it had been shortlisted for Orange fiction in 2008 which acted as a concluding factor. It turned out to be very beneficial as not only did I really enjoy reading the novel but the last few pages of the book contained an interview with its author. It was her first book and I found some of what she said about her style of writing very encouraging for me and my ideas about writing a first book. Particularly the epilogue section titled "Putting together a Robot without an Instruction Manual", comparing nuts and bolts with phrases and sentences.